TAKE IT EASY
BEFORE DINNER

Take It Easy
Before Dinner

RUTH LANGLAND HOLBERG

NEW YORK

Thomas Y. Crowell Company

For MARJORIE and WILLIAM ROSE BENÉT

and MELINNA and HARRISON CADY

Acknowledgments

I am deeply indebted to Marjorie Benét, Melinna Cady, Ann Roe Robbins, Virginia Lee Burton and George Demetrious for help in the assembling and testing of these recipes. I take this opportunity to thank the many other friends who have been interested in this collection. They are too numerous to mention by name.

INTRODUCTION

I BELIEVE that the hour before dinner should be gracious and peaceful with no creaking of domestic machinery, or frequent and frantic trips to the kitchen. This is the time when menfolks are home from work and the time when the best | HUSBAND | meal of the day should be planned for their pleasure. Men enjoy a cocktail or a quiet chat with an unhurried companion. They like to listen to the radio and make informative remarks on the news to the lady of their choice. If you don't agree with his views, save your comments for after dinner. A man's disposition after a good meal is enormously improved.

If you are having a party and the guests are present, you can be as calm and relaxed as though a battery of efficient maids were in charge of the kitchen. The well-known panic of wondering whether the dinner will be successful and | GUESTS | whether the guests will enjoy the evening will be eased off if you are not scrambling around the kitchen with one eye on the clock and the other on the food you are preparing. To be cook, hostess and waitress and to preserve tranquillity is not impossible if you know that nothing in the kitchen needs your attention this last hour. You can receive your guests and stay with them until cocktails are over.

For everyday living these recipes will suit the clubwoman or give a free afternoon for a matinee, shopping or charity work. They will suit the career woman or the woman who has a maid mornings only. A part-time maid can prepare | EVERYDAY | things ahead of time if you have her use this book. If you are an author, painter, musician or teacher, this is the book for you. It sounds like a sales talk, you say. Well, it is. You will find that these recipes really work.

If you have babies, it is possible for this hour to be given to

> BABIES

putting the infants to bed. Small children in the family can be given this time for reading and repeating their prayers, with your undivided attention.

Are you a working girl or a busy executive wondering how you can find time to entertain guests at dinner? These recipes are designed for you. Many of these dishes can be made the night be-

> WORKING GIRL

fore, kept in the refrigerator and baked or reheated with no bothersome watching. Long, slow cooking develops and blends flavors. All dishes that need high heat and fast cooking are left out of this book. There will be no smoke from the broiler and no smell of chops permeating the small apartment the night you are having guests. This is the complaint of one of my friends. That's why she says she is all agog waiting for this book.

The secret of leisure simply is careful planning. My method of giving a dinner party is this. Several days beforehand I write down a menu suitable to the time of the year, my finances (usu-

> METHOD

ally low) and what the markets have to offer. I look over my collection of recipes and, after selecting a main dish, I check over my supplies on hand and make a list of what to buy. If I am increasing the recipe to serve eight or more instead of four, I multiply carefully because I am an idiot at figures.

It has been a hobby of mine to collect recipes from the magazines, newspapers and my friends. They are filed in stout envelopes that once brought me a monthly poetry magazine. The women's magazines print delectable streamlined recipes that you should clip for your files. The food ads are worth reading and all their free booklets are an addition to the cook's library. Experts on the radio give you all sorts of good ideas.

I make out a menu that can be prepared a day before or during the morning of the day. I have never been able to give an entire day to party preparations. I have too many other irons in

| HERE'S HOW |

the fire. I set the table during the afternoon for a sit-down or a buffet meal. Dishes to be used in serving are laid out on the kitchen table. The dessert dishes and silver are ready, the tray of coffee cups, the tray of cocktail glasses and a bowl for cocktail crackers are arranged. Coffee is measured into the drip pot. Water for it will be set boiling when the dessert is being taken in from the kitchen. Everything that should be chilled—tomato juice, fruit juice, butter, the salad etc.—is in the refrigerator.

When greens arrive from the store they should be washed, drained and patted partly dry with a dish towel. A head of lettuce soaked in ice water, the core removed, then kept in a covered

| GREENS |

dish, will stay fresh and crisp for an amazingly long time. The same goes for celery. Other greens are stored in a covered pan in the refrigerator. Keep parsley and watercress in covered jars after they have been washed. The salad for dinner can be mixed and kept in a covered bowl. But for goodness' sake, don't add the dressing until time to serve it, or the greens will wilt.

Make a large jar of French dressing and keep it in the refrigera-

| FRENCH DRESSING |

tor. A clove of garlic should repose in its depths. Shake well before using. A refrigerator can do a lot of work for you. Be sure to let it.

Vegetables can be prepared during odd moments. The main

| ODDS AND ENDS |

dish has been made ready and is either waiting to be baked, reheated or assembled. Rolls are in a paper bag to be heated a few minutes in the oven. Look around and check up on everything.

Now, this is important for your peace of mind and an uncluttered kitchen. There should not be an unwashed dish or pan in the kitchen. Clean up as you go along. Now you can put on your party dress and relax.

This is a very personal and informal cook book. The recipes have been tried many times. They are designed for four or six people as a rule, but they can be increased to serve twelve or sixteen people with very little more work than is needed to prepare for four.

INCREASING
RECIPES

When you are having guests for dinner, delegate one of the men to help you. Let your husband remain at the table chatting with the guests. It causes less flurry and your helper is flattered. He can carry the plates and silver to the kitchen where you scrape, rinse and stack neatly.

GUEST
HELP

Get the dessert ready for him to carry in to the table. Pour boiling water in the drip coffee pot and join your guests, bringing in the coffee tray at the same time. Perhaps you missed some good jokes and witty remarks, but your guests are having a good time. It looks as if the party were a success.

DESSERT
AND COFFEE

Finally, you say when the last drop of coffee has been sipped, "Let's find more comfortable chairs." Men get restless if kept too long in the same chair. Or else, serve coffee in another room from a low table. Someone takes the last dishes to the kitchen. You scrape, rinse and stack them and put away leftovers. I hope you have a little mirror in the kitchen with a lipstick and some face powder. Make a few repairs if your face needs it. Turn out the light and proceed to enjoy the rest of the evening as much as you did the first.

Those stacked dishes can be washed in a jiffy when the party is over. It is fun to talk over the evening with your husband and to hear the stories you missed while you were out of the room. Your husband will hardly know he is drying the dishes, especially after a jolly evening.

DISH WASHING

KEEP ON HAND

Biscuit mixes, muffin mixes, cake and pie mixes.

Pudding and gelatines in packages.

Cinnamon, nutmeg, mace, cloves, allspice, ginger, mustard.

| ADD IMAGINATION TO THESE | Vanilla, lemon, orange, mint and almond extracts. Celery salt, celery seeds, onion and garlic salts, curry powder, chili powder, parsley flakes. |

Dehydrated sauces, such as mushroom, spaghetti, white and brown.

Examine the grocer's shelves for new products and try all short cuts.

Do a lot of canning and preserving or else buy relishes, jams, jellies, chutney and chili sauce.

There are many sets of herbs with directions for use. The most valuable to me are tarragon, basil, thyme, dill, parsley and chives. There are some mixtures suitable for meat dishes or cheese dishes and there are soup bags for different kinds of soups.

Doughnuts, cakes, cookies and pies bought from a fine bakery will save baking. Ice cream and sherbet are perfect desserts. I have included a few of my favorite desserts.

| A SUGGESTION | Buy good coffee and serve it hot or iced with every dinner. |

Every now and then have an old-fashioned baking day and turn out a batch of cookies or a fat layer cake with a delicate filling and frosted to perfection. Make a pie and keep some pastry in the refrigerator for another day.

How about a special coffee cake or fancy bread or tiny rolls? And by all means, bake bread. The delectable aroma of bread baking is wonderful in a house and homemade bread is wonderful to eat, too.

Contents

BEEF

PORK

VEAL

LAMB

FOWL

FISH

CHOWDERS

VEGETABLES

EGGS

CHEESE

BREAD

DESSERTS

xviii CONTENTS

TAKE IT EASY
BEFORE DINNER

Beef Stroganoff

THERE are as many varieties of Beef Stroganoff as there are Swedish Meatballs. This recipe uses chopped beef and is really very good.

First fry 2 chopped onions in 3 tablespoons of fat until pale yellow. Stir in 2 tablespoons of flour, add gradually 1 cup of stock or 1 cup of water with a beef bouillon cube dissolved in it. Cook until smooth. Add 1 tablespoon of tomato paste or tomato catsup, I teaspoon Worcestershire sauce, ½ teaspoon salt, ⅛ teaspoon pepper. Simmer and stir for 10 minutes.

In another frying pan brown 1 pound of chopped beef. If the beef has much fat in it, have the pan hot and the fat will fry out. If the meat is free from fat, use a bit of fat in the pan to keep it from sticking. Stir with a fork to prevent lumping. Add meat to the thickened sauce.

Now, gently fry ½ pound of sliced mushrooms in the pan in which the meat was cooked, until tender or about 10 minutes. Add mushrooms to the meat mixture. If you wish to serve this dish hours later, put it aside and, when you heat it later, add 1 cup of sour cream. Heat again, but do not let it come to a boil.

The sour cream does something heavenly to the meat and mushrooms. 6 people will "lick the platter clean."

Swedish Meatballs from Minnesota

1 POUND of ground beef, or veal, or beef and pork mixed, ground 3 times! Mix the meat with 1 teaspoon salt, a sprinkle of pepper and a scant teaspoon of sugar.

Stir in gradually ½ cup of milk and ⅓ cup of bread crumbs dissolved in an additional ½ cup of milk. Now add 1 medium-sized potato cooked and mashed. Mix very well until fluffy and the mixture sticks to the bottom of the bowl. Then add 1 teaspoon of onion minced and fried in 1 teaspoon of butter.

Form into small balls, tidbit size, and fry in 3 or 4 tablespoons of butter or margarine. Take out the browned meatballs and heat a gravy in the same pan. You do this by adding 3 tablespoons of flour which have been dissolved into ½ cup of water. As soon as this is smooth, pour in 1 cup of hot water with 2 bouillon cubes dissolved in it. Continue to cook and stir until smooth. If the gravy is not a good dark brown, add a few drops of Kitchen Bouquet.

If you wish to serve this later, wait until then to combine meatballs and gravy and heat gently over a low flame. This is plenty for 4 people.

Of all the meatballs I have tasted, these are the most delicate and make a grand buffet dish in a casserole.

Easy Tamale Pie

IN A large frying pan brown 1½ pounds of chopped beef and 1 large onion, sliced. Add 1 can of condensed tomato soup, 1 teaspoon salt, ¼ teaspoon pepper, 3 tablespoons chili powder (or less), ½ cup of chopped ripe olives and a 12-ounce can of whole-kernel corn.

Pour this into a rather flat, greased baking dish and bake 1½ hours in a 325 degree oven. Make a corn bread mixture by using a package of prepared corn muffin mix, following the directions for corn bread on the package. Spread the corn bread batter on top of the baked meat mixture and bake 25 minutes longer in a hotter oven, 425 degrees.

But if you wish to prepare this Tamale Pie in the morning, follow directions up to the corn bread. Then forget about it until

¾ of an hour before dinner. Do not, however, leave it in a hot oven all this time. Reheat in the oven about 15 minutes. Meanwhile, prepare the corn bread and spread it on top of the hot meat. This takes only a few minutes. The dish will then bake with no attention from the cook for 25 minutes in the oven preheated to 425 degrees.

8 portions is the yield, as many recipes announce. I would rather say 8 persons will have plenty to eat from this recipe. Using the word "portions" gives me the impression that no one is going to eat and beg for second helpings of the cook's *pièce de résistance.*

New Canaan Meat Loaf

THIS meat loaf is a stand-by in the home of a friend who writes cook books and she has given the recipe to me for this book. It can be prepared during the day.

2 pounds of mixed ground pork and veal—more veal than pork —are mixed with 3 stalks of celery diced fine, 1 onion diced, some parsley and 1 cup of soft bread crumbs. Season with ½ cup of catsup or homemade chili sauce, 1 teaspoon Worcestershire sauce, 1 teaspoon salt, ¼ teaspoon pepper. Add one beaten egg. Mix well and shape into a loaf or pack into a greased bread pan. Bake for 1 hour in an oven heated to 350 degrees.

A mushroom sauce is often served with this loaf but it isn't necessary. The mushroom sauce is a can of mushroom soup, undiluted except for a tablespoon of cream. The loaf is good cold for sandwiches.

Carter's Hamburg Special

THIS is the answer for one of those days so crowded with activity that you never had a moment to do a thing about dinner. You have a pound of hamburg in the refrigerator. Season it well with salt and pepper and a few drops of onion juice—no solid bits of onion this time.

Toast bread and butter it well. If your family likes meat rare, toast 4 slices of bread. Divide the meat into 4 parts and spread it on the toasted bread to the edges. Pop the slices under the broiler and cook to your own taste.

If the family of 4 prefer their meat well done, toast 8 slices of bread, butter them well. Spread each slice with ⅛ of the meat and broil until done to a turn.

Have the family help you with this meal. Let them choose anything on the emergency shelf they want to accompany the sizzling hamburgs. Pile everything on trays and eat in any room you prefer, or on the porch or in the back yard. Have fun with the meal. The Carters do. This is Damon Carter's own invention.

Swedish Meatballs

GRIND 1 pound of chopped beef and ⅓ pound of lean pork twice. If the butcher grinds it once for you, and refuses to grind it again, do it yourself the second time. It makes a great deal of difference in the result. Mix the ground meat with 1 beaten egg, ⅓ cup of dry bread crumbs, a little grated onion—not over 2 teaspoons of onion—1 teaspoon salt, ⅛ teaspoon of pepper and a pinch of nutmeg.

Whip the mixture vigorously in a bowl until quite smooth. Form in tiny balls, roll them in flour and brown in 2 tablespoons of fat.

Add water almost to cover the balls and simmer 15 minutes. Remove to a casserole. Make gravy in the pan adding more water to make 2 cups of gravy. A few drops of Kitchen Bouquet give color and flavor. Pour the gravy over the meatballs and allow to cool if you are not serving the dish at once. You may let it stand in the refrigerator until dinner time if the weather is very hot.

Heat in the oven half an hour before serving. This dish improves and I have known Swedes to make enough for days at a time, declaring the flavor improved every day.

A week of meatballs does not appeal to me. Two days is plenty.

Mushroom Stew with Meatballs

FOR the stew, sauté 2 pounds of sliced mushrooms in 3 tablespoons of fat in a large frying pan until tender. Stir in 3 tablespoons of flour and gradually add 1½ cups of water. Cook until thick, stirring diligently. Now add 2 teaspoons of beef extract, ¼ cup of lemon juice, 1 teaspoon salt and a shaking of pepper. Simmer 5 minutes.

In another pan fry 1 finely chopped, medium-sized onion until pale yellow, in 1 tablespoon of fat. Then moisten 1⅓ cups of soft bread crumbs with a very little water, add to ¾ pound of chopped beef. Mix with the fried onion and roll into tiny balls; you should be able to make 18. Brown the meatballs in 2 tablespoons of fat. Add them to the mushroom stew and simmer for 20 minutes.

This stew will feed 6 people and it may be set aside for hours and heated just before serving time. Flavors blend and develop during the waiting.

Scalloped Cheeseburger

THIS is one of the best chopped beef variations that I know and it can be prepared and left waiting until 30 minutes before time to eat it. For a buffet supper it is a favorite with the men.

Peel and dice 6 medium-sized potatoes, cook in a small amount of boiling salted water until tender. Drain, but save the potato water and add enough milk to it to make 2 cups.

Melt ¼ cup of butter or margarine and add ¼ cup of flour. Stir until smooth and gradually add the liquid. Cook and stir until thick and smooth, about 5 minutes. Season with salt and paprika. Add the potatoes and pour into a greased baking dish.

You have a pound of chopped beef to season with salt and pepper. Shape it into 6 flat cakes. Place the meat cakes around the edge of the baking dish and sprinkle a cup of grated cheese over the entire top. Bake in a moderate oven, 375 degrees for half an hour or until the surface is nice and brown. 6 persons empty the dish.

Tamale Pie

FRY 2 sliced onions and a minced clove of garlic in 2 tablespoons of fat until light brown. Add 1 pound of chopped beef and continue frying, stirring frequently. Add 2 teaspoons of salt, 1 tablespoon of chili powder. Use more if you like a very hot dish. Add a large can of tomatoes, 1 cup of seedless raisins, 1 cup of pitted or sliced ripe olives. Simmer slowly for 1½ hours.

Meanwhile, slowly stir 2 cups of cornmeal into 6 cups of boiling water, with 2 teaspoons of salt and 2 teaspoons of chili powder. Cook over low heat for 15 minutes, stirring often. When this cornmeal mush is cooked, line the sides and bottom of a 2-quart casserole or baking dish with a layer of the mush. Pour in the meat filling. Spread the rest of the mush over the top. Bake in a slow oven 325 degrees for 1½ hours.

I sometimes add a cup of canned whole-kernel corn or fresh corn, cooked kidney beans or shell beans to the meat filling. Some like cheese sprinkled on the top 15 minutes before removing from the oven.

This will serve 6 people. It can be made the day before and re-heated, in fact some recipes demand that treatment in order to produce a blend of flavors. This is a wonderful party dish for it can be doubled and tripled with no extra work.

Hamburg Patties with Roquefort Spread

THE ever-popular hamburg patties are given a new and surprising zest with a quickly gotten together sauce.

Four people make quick work of a pound of hamburg put through the chopper twice. If your butcher refuses to do it or is too busy, get out your own chopper for the second grinding. Season the meat with salt and pepper and divide it into 8 thin patties about 4 or 5 inches in diameter. Lay each patty on a piece of heavy waxed paper and stack them and put in the refrigerator until wanted.

Mash 3 tablespoons of Roquefort cheese. A fork does the work well unless the cheese is very dry. Nothing but the food chopper will do the mashing in that case. Cream the cheese with 3 tablespoons of butter or margarine and 1 tablespoon of prepared mustard. Add a few drops of A1 or Worcestershire sauce and a little salt and pepper. Beat until well mixed and fluffy. Minced chives are wonderful in the sauce if you have some in the garden or growing in the kitchen window, but this is up to your liking. This sauce can be left at room temperature.

A few minutes before dinner, lay the hamburg patties on a cooky tin and pop under the broiler. They cook through in a very short time. Just before taking from the broiler spread a dab of the cheese sauce on each patty and allow them to remain under the broiler for a jiffy. Then serve at once.

These are grand for picnics with toasted buns. You could have toasted buns for dinner, come to think of it.

Stuffed Cabbage

USE outside leaves of a cabbage and wilt them by boiling 5 minutes in hot water. 8 large leaves are about right. Much depends on the size of the leaf.

Wash 1 tablespoon of rice and boil it in hot water for 10 minutes. Drain. Mix with 1 pound of chopped beef, 1 teaspoon salt, 1 teaspoon paprika, 1 teaspoon onion juice. Beat 1 egg and add it to the meat. Mix very well and divide into 8 rolls that will fit a cabbage leaf and will be neatly hidden in the rolled leaf. I stick them with a toothpick to keep from unrolling. Some use heavy thread to make little bundles. Place in a large frying pan or kettle and put in 1 pound of sauerkraut, 1 onion minced and 1 tomato cut up or 1 cup of canned tomatoes; add enough hot water to cover. Cover pan and cook slowly 1½ hours.

Rub 2 tablespoons of flour into 2 tablespoons of bacon fat. Pour a little of the liquid on this and stir until thick. Add it to the liquid in the big kettle and cook until smooth and thick.

This is one of those dishes that develops more flavor if allowed to stand at the back of the stove most of the day. Bring rapidly to a steaming heat and serve. 4 or 5 people will have plenty.

American Chop Suey

THIS is a wonderful meal for youngsters. Let them have a party for a couple of their friends. It can be prepared in the morning by the youngsters and they can go off swimming or skating and come home to a cosy kitchen and a whole meal that needs only a quick heating to bring it to a flavorsome perfection.

Cook ½ pound of elbow macaroni according to directions on the package. Drain. While this is cooking, brown 1 pound of hamburg in 1 teaspoon of fat, along with 1 onion finely minced. Season with 1 teaspoon salt, ⅛ teaspoon pepper. Add 2 cans of condensed tomato soup. Stir until well mixed. Add the drained and cooked macaroni and simmer over a low heat for ½ hour, stirring now and then. Set aside to blend and ripen.

Bring to a bubbling heat just before meal time. This will serve 4. The recipe can be increased with no more effort than it takes to serve. Watch the youngsters go for it.

Russian Steak

I DON'T know of a tastier treatment for bottom of the round. Buy 2 pounds of bottom of the round, but if your butcher tells you top of round is better, agree with him, take it and pay a bit more.

Trim off the skin and fat. Pound the meat on a heavy paper, and save washing a board. The pounding is usually done with a regular meat pounder that looks like a mallet and has the ends of the mallet corrugated either in ridges or points. The bottom of a milk bottle will do the trick. Pound in flour, salt and pepper, as you pound. The meat seems to absorb the flour. Cut in 2-inch squares.

In the meantime, have 2 cups of chopped onions browning lightly in 4 tablespoons of bacon fat. This will take 25 to 30 minutes over a slow fire. Don't try to hurry the onions.

Remove the onions from the pan and leave as much fat as possible in the pan. Brown the meat in it. To fit each piece in the pan you will need a large frying pan for 2 pounds of meat. Sprinkle with flour and a little more salt and pepper. When brown, turn and repeat, sprinkling flour on this side. Now add the onions and 2 cups of hot water. Bring to a bubbling boil. Cover and turn flame low so that only a gentle simmering goes on for 1 hour.

Now, scrape up from the bottom of the pan whatever flour seems to have stuck, add 1 cup of sour cream. Cover again and cook slowly until the meat is very tender. Bottom of the round will take an hour longer. Let stand until ready for dinner if you are not serving it at once.

When dinner time approaches, heat the meat for about 10 minutes, and if you are wise you have boiled some little new potatoes that you can tuck into the pan to heat with the meat.

This amount will serve 5 or 6 people.

Boneless Birds

THIS has long been one of my favorites. It has infinite variations.

Persuade the butcher to cut round steak or veal as thin as possible. 1 pound of round steak or veal should make four rolls, so cut the slice into four squares.

Make a stuffing by sautéing 3 tablespoons of finely minced onion, 3 tablespoons of celery and 1 tablespoon parsley. Toss in after 5 or 6 minutes 1½ cups of soft bread crumbs. Season with ¼ teaspoon salt and a dash of pepper. If you like herbs, add a pinch of your favorite. It may be thyme, tarragon, savoury or basil. Mix well. Remove from heat.

Divide the stuffing between the four slices of steak or veal. Heap it up in the center. Roll and wrap in a strip of bacon and fasten with a toothpick or tie with string.

Brown the rolls in a hot frying pan. The bacon will provide the fat. When brown, add 1½ cups of hot water in which a beef bouillon cube has been dissolved, and 1 teaspoon Worcestershire sauce. Cover closely and allow to simmer 45 minutes. If you are planning to use this dish for dinner some hours later, remove the rolls, or boneless birds, and make a gravy in the pan by mixing 2 tablespoons of flour with 3 tablespoons of cold water stirred smooth with a fork. Pour slowly into the liquid and cook until thick. Remove from heat. Put the rolls back, cover again and forget it until 15 or 20 minutes before dinner. Heat gently and serve with boiled noodles or mashed potatoes. This will feed 4 very well.

The stuffing may be pepped up with a sliver of dill pickle, a cooked prune or an olive. You may use tomato, either canned or in paste form instead of the beef bouillon. The use of tomato paste changes the name of the dish to Red Birds.

Savory Round Steak

MARINATE a 2-pound slice of bottom of the round in ¾ cup of Burgundy wine, ½ clove of garlic, 1 chopped onion, a pinch each of powdered origanum and marjoram, 1 teaspoon celery flakes, ¼ teaspoon of pepper. Set the dish in the refrigerator, cover with wax paper.

This should be marinating as long as you find convenient— several hours or overnight. During the time allowed, turn the beef over once.

Heat fat. I use the trimmings of beef fat tried out. Rub flour into the meat, brown well on each side. Add 1 teaspoon of salt and ⅛ teaspoon of pepper and the strained wine from the marinating bath.

If you wish to bake this in a covered casserole, set the oven at 275 degrees and bake for 3 hours.

You can simmer this on a low flame for several hours, or until the meat is tender. I had a very tough piece of utility beef and this treatment is warranted to break down the resistance of the toughest piece of meat. Make gravy with the liquid left in the pan. If there is not enough, use beef bouillon cubes dissolved in hot water.

Rulle Polse

MY NORWEGIAN sister-in-law taught me this trick with flank steak. It is a Christmas meat and when sliced between slabs of Jule Kage (Christmas Bread to you), it is something to rave about.

You must allow at least 6 days if you want it for Christmas Eve. Buy a flank steak from the butcher. If the hard skin has not been pulled off, ask him to do it for you. Most flank steaks are ready for use nowadays.

Spread out the steak. If it seems too thick in places to roll up tightly, slice off the humps and place the strips of meat crosswise on the steak. Cover with finely chopped onions, 1 teaspoon salt and ½ teaspoon pepper, ½ teaspoon ginger, ⅛ teaspoon saltpeter. You buy the last ingredient in a drug store, it is a preservative.

Roll tightly and bind with lots of string around and around. Ragna even sewed cheesecloth around the rolls.

Now you make a brine of 3 quarts of water, 1 cup of coarse salt, ½ cup of brown sugar, ⅛ teaspoon saltpeter. Boil together a few minutes. Cool. Put roll in and let stand 6 days with a weight on to keep under the brine.

At the end of 6 days, put the roll in a kettle and cover with cold water and let it simmer over a slow fire about 3 hours. It should be very tender then. When done, remove from kettle and press between 2 plates with a weight on the top plate.

This is really very little work. The roll keeps in the refrigerator for 2 weeks. You may have other rolls in the brine and take them out any time after the six days. There is enough meat in 1 roll, sliced thin, for 8 or 10 people.

A typical Norwegian Christmas Eve supper boasts of this Rulle Polse, along with the Fish pudding, the Lutefisk, the Sildesalat and other tidbits. But you start with rice pudding surrounded with a red fruit juice sauce or else sprinkled with sugar and cinnamon with a huge chunk of butter dreaming its life away in the middle of the creamy rice.

I always have a plate of potet Kage. Easy to do and interesting to eat. My Norwegian grandmother always had them for Sunday coffee, from 3 to 4 o'clock, and we loved it. Especially the Kavring that we dunked in weak coffee and brought up dripping to be plastered at the immediate instant with a piece of butter and popped into the mouth. Kavring are sweet biscuits a day old, cut in half and toasted in a very slow oven.

The potato cakes are simply cold mashed potatoes mixed with enough flour to make a stiff dough. Roll quite thin into pancakes. Bake on top of the coal stove or on an ungreased pancake griddle until brown blisters appear. Turn to the other side. Eat, spread with butter, sugar and cinnamon or jelly. Roll them up or fold into wedges. They are eaten cold.

Deviled Round Steak

Buy 1½ or 2 pounds of round steak, top or bottom of the round, have it cut 1½ inches thick. Score it deeply with a sharp knife and brush with 1 teaspoon of mustard spread.

Mix well 4 tablespoons chili sauce, 3 tablespoons melted butter or margarine, 1 teaspoon salt, 1 teaspoon Worcestershire sauce, ¼ teaspoon pepper, ¼ teaspoon paprika, 1 tablespoon grated onion and 4 tablespoons of lemon juice.

Marinate the steak in this sauce for at least 2 hours, turning it over occasionally.

Cut the stems from ½ pound of mushrooms and chop them coarsely. Stuff the tops with well seasoned bread stuffing. Remove steak from the sauce and brown it on both sides in 2 tablespoons of fat in a hot frying pan.

Mix the sauce with 1 cup of hot water and pour it over the steak. Add the chopped mushroom stems also. Cover and cook slowly 45 to 60 minutes. The steak should be very tender, if it is not, cook a little longer.

Fry the mushroom caps in 2 tablespoons butter or margarine until they turn dark, about 10 or 15 minutes.

If you wish to have this steak later in the day, set it aside and lay the stuffed mushrooms on the top. 20 minutes before serving time, start a low flame under the frying pan and allow the steak to heat gently. The gravy in the pan may be thickened if you desire.

This treatment turns a tough piece of beef to something a gourmet will praise. A 2-pound steak will serve 5 or 6.

Meat Pie

IF YOU have roast beef leftover, or any other cold cooked meat you can give it a first-appearance look if you concoct this meat pie. Best of all, you fix it in the morning and have the day free for other duties or pleasures.

For a family of 5 or 6, you need 1½ to 2 cups of cubed cold meat. Peel and cube 3 medium-sized potatoes. Slice 4 carrots, chop 1 onion. If you have fresh peas, shell enough for ½ cup. Cook these vegetables in ½ cup of water and 1 teaspoon salt until just tender. Cover the pan while they are cooking. Add the meat to the cooked vegetables and season with your favorite herbs. A pinch or whiff of rosemary marjoram and a dash of black pepper is just right. Pour in 1 cup of gravy. Mix gently and pour into a greased casserole. Cover with pie crust and cut little slits in the top so the steam can escape. If you are pressed for time, use a packaged pastry mix. Now place the casserole in the refrigerator and forget it until 30 minutes before dinner time.

Have the oven hot first. A temperature of 425 degrees is right. Bake 30 minutes or until the crust is brown.

Singhalese Dinner

THIS is one of my favorite dinners. For 6 people I buy 1½ pounds of round steak. Cut the meat in small cubes and brown it in 2 tablespoons of fat. I try out the trimmings of the steak and use the fat to brown the meat. When the meat has been turned to brown on all sides, add 1 large onion and 1 sweet pepper cut up, a clove of garlic and 1 bay leaf. Let these fry gently at one side of the pan if there is room. If not, brown them in another pan. To this mixture add 2 or 3 tablespoons of curry powder according to your taste, 1 teaspoon of paprika, 1 teaspoon ginger, 1 teaspoon cinnamon, 1 teaspoon salt, 2 chopped tomatoes, 2 chopped apples and 1 cup of milk. If the milk does not cover the meat add enough water to make up amount of liquid needed. Then add the juice of a lemon and allow the pan to simmer very slowly until the meat is tender and well done. Now and then stir the mixture and add more water if it seems to be cooking away. You want to have about 2 cups of liquid, for this gravy is very good. You may thicken it with a little flour and water.

This curry, like all curries, improves with standing. Make it in the morning or the day before. Serve it with boiled rice.

Now comes the surprising accompaniment to the dinner. Chop a small cabbage finely and boil in a little water until soft. Drain. Add ½ teaspoon of turmeric, 2 teaspoons butter or margarine, salt to taste and ½ package of shredded coconut. Mix well. Set aside, and before dinner heat it in a double boiler. People who do not like cabbage take to this unusual dish with gusto.

Now slice 2 Spanish onions into rings, separate them, sprinkle with 1 teaspoon of salt, 2 teaspoons of sugar, ½ teaspoon of turmeric, ¼ teaspoon pepper. Squeeze enough lemon juice over all to coat the onion rings. Let the salad stand several hours to ripen.

If you are hot on the trail of food adventures, try Samball.

Mix shredded coconut with a pinch of cayenne pepper, enough lemon juice and cream to make a paste. Pat it into cake form and serve as a relish with the Singhalese dinner.

Curried potatoes are sometimes served with the meat and rice.

Dice 5 or 6 medium-sized potatoes, boil in a small amount of water and drain. Add 1 finely chopped onion, 1 clove of garlic (or less), 1 teaspoon butter or margarine, ½ teaspoon turmeric and 2 teaspoons of curry powder. Use less if you want a delicately flavored result.

Cover with boiled milk and simmer until the onion and garlic are merged with the potatoes. Serve hot.

I always follow this highly seasoned dinner with a cool pineapple dessert.

Chili Con Carne

CUT 2 pounds of round steak into cubes, not over ½ inch, and discard all tough edges. You want each bite to be free from skin or fat when you eat this dish of meat and chili powder.

Brown the diced beef in 2 tablespoons of either beef or bacon fat. In another pan brown 2½ cups of chopped onions in 2 tablespoons of fat. If you have a green pepper, and you should, cut it in thin rings and brown lightly with the onions. Combine meat and onions in a large frying pan or kettle. Add 2 tablespoons of chili powder, 2 teaspoons of salt, 1 teaspoon sugar, a clove of garlic slivered and a few grains of cayenne. Pour over this 3½ cups of canned tomatoes and 2 cups of hot water. Cover and cook slowly 1 hour. Stir now and then.

Open a can of red kidney beans and add them to the meat. Cook slowly about half an hour. The meat should be very tender by this time. It may be served at once but the flavors improve with a few hours or even overnight. Bring it to a bubbling boil. There should be plenty of liquid so that mounds of mashed potatoes or boiled rice may be inundated with glowing rosy streams studded with tender cubes of beef. 6 may be fed with this recipe or it may stretch to 8. This is one of those elastic stews that delights a hostess for she may at the last minute invite another guest.

Beef with Red Wine

CUT into small cubes 2 pounds of lean stewing beef and brown in 2 tablespoons of fat. Take out the meat and in the fat remaining in the pan stir 1 tablespoon of flour until free from lumps. Add 1 teaspoon salt, ¼ teaspoon pepper and 1½ cups of dry red wine. Stir until smooth.

In a small saucepan lightly brown 5 or 6 small onions, sliced, using 1 tablespoon butter or margarine. Put them in the wine gravy along with the brown cubes of beef, 1 carrot sliced, ½ cup of mushrooms and some garden herbs. If you are not familiar with herbs, use a few sprigs of parsley, thyme and half a bay leaf.

If you are fond of lamb kidneys, this is the dish they will improve. 6 kidneys should be washed, split and skinned and fat removed. Soak in cold, salted water 1 hour. Drain and slice thin. All this is done before you start to brown the beef.

Add the sliced lamb kidneys to the other ingredients. There should be enough liquid in the kettle almost to cover the meat. Have the flame under the kettle low and allow it to simmer gently 3 or 4 hours. Be sure the lid fits closely on the kettle. An iron Dutch Oven is perfect or if you know how to handle a casserole on top of the stove, it is also suitable.

Half an hour before dinner time, pour in a liqueur glass of brandy. That is, if you have the brandy.

The absolute tenderness of the meat and the rich dark gravy is something to rave about. Boiled rice that has dried off in the oven so that each grain is separate, is just right with the meat and gravy.

This recipe with the lamb kidneys will feed 8 people. Without the kidneys it will feed 6.

Roast Beef

SEVERAL people have tested this method of roasting beef. It makes it possible to have a roast for Sunday dinner and still have time for church or a walk in the country.

The idea is to roast the beef ⅔ of the time required. You figure out how much time each pound needs. Beef rare needs 18 to 20 minutes per pound. Beef medium needs 22 to 25 minutes per pound and beef well-done needs 27 to 30 minutes per pound. The oven temperature should be 300 degrees.

A rib or sirloin roast should be room temperature. Trim off extra fat and hard edges. Wipe with a damp cloth. Sprinkle with salt and pepper. If you like garlic, rub the surface with a cut clove of garlic. Dredge with flour, and place fat side up in an open pan. If the roast is very lean lay strips of suet over the top.

A rolled roast is treated the same way but it needs more time— about 5 or 10 minutes longer per pound.

You may brown the roast for 20 minutes in a very hot oven 500 degrees, if you wish. Then turn the heat to 300 degrees. Roast for ⅔ of the time you have figured your particular piece of beef needs. Baste now and then with drippings in the pan. Turn off heat. Let stand.

Allow the oven to heat to 300 degrees when you are getting ready for dinner. Finish roasting.

I hope this is all clear. I figure out the problem of pounds and minutes on a piece of paper and divide the sum into three parts. Two parts for the first roasting time and one part for the heating and finishing before dinner. I keep the paper where I can see it and watch the clock at the same time.

Pot Roast

EVERYONE has a special seasoning for pot roast. This recipe is a very good one and the seasonings can be altered to suit your own liking, but I have found this combination excellent.

Buy a chunk of beef, rump, chuck or whatever the butcher has to offer. 4 or 5 pounds is about right for a family of 6.

Trim any fat from the meat and try it out in the frying pan. Remove the crisp bits.

Mix 2 tablespoons of flour, 1 tablespoon brown sugar, ½ teaspoon dry mustard, 2 teaspoons of salt and your special herb mixture. If you have none, use 2 teaspoons of poultry seasoning. Rub this into the meat and brown it in the fat with 1 sliced onion. When the beef is brown on all sides, add 1 cup of hot water, cover the pan and simmer over a low flame for 3 or 4 hours. Now and then lift the cover to see if it needs more water to keep it from sticking or cooking dry. It probably will.

One hour before serving, tuck in 8 carrots cut in half the long way, 8 small peeled onions and 8 medium-sized potatoes. When done, remove to a heated platter and thicken the liquid in the pan. You should have at least 2 cups, with 2 tablespoons of flour mixed smooth with a little water. It is a good idea when adding the vegetables to add more water if you think you are not going to come out at the end with at least 2 cups of stock in the pan.

This pot roast simmers along placidly during the day with very little attention, in fact it can be finished hours before dinner time and simply brought to a good rousing heat in about 10 or 15 minutes.

This will feed a family of 6.

Braised Short Ribs of Beef

YEARS ago this was a favorite of mine in a famous Chicago hotel. Of course, beef in the Middle West is about the best the country offers.

Cut 2 pounds of beef short ribs into pieces right for serving. Flour them well and brown slowly in a hot frying pan in 2 tablespoons of lard. This will take 20 to 30 minutes. Add 2 teaspoons of salt, ¼ teaspoon pepper, ½ an onion minced and ½ cup of hot water. Cover and simmer over a low flame for 2 hours. If you keep the flame low and if the cover fits closely you will not need to look at it during the 2 hours.

You may set it aside if you wish to finish cooking later in the day. Whichever way you choose, allow at least 40 minutes to finish cooking. Add 2 carrots cut in slivers, 2 stalks of celery cut in short slivers and 1 green pepper sliced in thin rings. Cook slowly for 40 minutes. Remove meat to platter and thicken the gravy with 1 tablespoon of flour stirred into ½ cup of water. Boil until smooth. This will serve 4 or 5.

Baked Tongue

THIS typical Norwegian Sunday dinner can be mostly prepared on Saturday. A fresh beef tongue covered with boiling water, lightly salted, needs to cook slowly until tender. This takes 3½ hours. Let it partially cool in the water. Peel off the skin and remove the roots while it is still warm. Then return it to the cooking water to cool.

An hour before dinner time place the tongue in a roasting pan. Have the temperature at 350 degrees. Pour 1 cup of tomato purée and 1 cup of sliced canned mushrooms over the tongue. Bake for 45 to 60 minutes.

A Norwegian housewife who is doubtless trying to impress the pastor invited for Sunday dinner, will serve potato molds with the baked tongue. They are fancy little affairs that can be fussed over during the morning if you have time, or even the day before.

You need 1½ cups of mashed potatoes, 6 tablespoons of cooked peas and 2 cooked carrots, if the carrots are large, or four small ones. First, butter a set of six muffin tins. Cut the carrots the height of the pans and cut into small lengthwise strips. Line the molds with carrot strips leaving ¼ inch between each strip. Place 1 tablespoon of peas in the bottom of each pan. Pack in ¼ cup of mashed potato.

If these molds are not to be served immediately, cover with wax paper to keep from drying out. To heat, place muffin tins in a pan of hot water until they are heated through. This takes 15 to 20 minutes depending on the thickness of the muffin tins. Unmold and place around the baked tongue and decorate with parsley.

A beef tongue serves at least 6 people. Any leftovers, minced or ground, add a gourmet touch to salads, omelets, or gelatin loaves calling for meat.

Baked Pork Chops

Cut off fat from 4 thick loin chops. Try out fat in skillet and brown the chops in the fat. Arrange the chops in a baking dish that will accommodate them without crowding. Place 1 tablespoon of raw rice on each chop. Mix a quart jar of canned tomatoes with 1 minced onion, 4 fresh basil leaves or ¼ teaspoon of dry leaves and a pinch of marjoram. Season with 1 teaspoon of salt, ⅓ teaspoon of pepper. Pour this around the chops, and dribble it over the rice. Add enough hot water to make the liquid almost cover the chops. Cover and cook in a slow oven 350 degress for 1 hour.

My special lemon pie gives a delicate finish to the heartiness of the meat dish.

Stuffed Pork Chops

Four people need a chop each. You ask for double, rib pork chops and have the butcher slit a pocket in each chop.

Make a dry bread stuffing. There is an excellent stuffing all ready to mix according to directions on the package. After filling the pockets, pin them shut with toothpicks. Sprinkle with flour, salt and pepper. Brown the chops in 2 tablespoons of hot fat until they have a good toasty color.

Place the chops in a pan with a close cover. Pour around them 1½ cups of hot water, a cup of sliced onions and bake in a moderate oven, 350 degrees, for 1½ hours. They need no attention during the baking.

You may stuff and brown the chops in the morning and have

them all ready to pop in the oven for the final cooking if you are busy during the day with other duties.

Pork Chops and Pineapple

Buy four double, rib pork chops and have the butcher make a slit in each chop. This pocket is to be stuffed with ¾ cup of crushed pineapple mixed with ½ teaspoon salt, ¼ teaspoon paprika, 2 tablespoons chopped parsley and a dash of black pepper. Pin shut with toothpicks.

Sprinkle the chops with salt and pepper and place on a trivet in an open roaster. Have the oven very hot, 500 degrees for 20 minutes. This will brown the chops. Turn down the heat to 300 degrees and continue the roasting for 1 hour and 10 minutes. There should be some fat in the pan to make gravy. Stir in 2 tablespoons of flour and when smooth, gradually add 2 cups of hot water in which 2 chicken or beef bouillon cubes have been dissolved. Cook until thick.

These stuffed pork chops require so little watching that you may start them 2 hours before dinner time and have the last hour free for other things.

Pork Chops, Harrison Cady Style

Sear as many pork chops as you need, one for each person. Cut the fat from the chops and let some of it sizzle in the frying pan. Put in the chops and turn to brown each side.

Take them out and lay them flat in a casserole. Sprinkle with salt and pepper. Place 3 cooked prunes on each chop and pour 1 cup of prune juice around the chops. This is enough juice for 4 or 5 chops.

Bake in a slow oven for an hour. A slow oven in this case is 300 degrees. With this dish baking and calling for no attention, you can go about doing other things.

Sweet potatoes in orange skins are nice to serve with the chops.

Save the breakfast orange halves. Clean out the membrane and wrap them in wax paper. Store in the icebox until you have enough.

Mash either canned or boiled sweet potatoes with enough hot milk to make them fluffy. Season with ⅛ teaspoon nutmeg, 1 tablespoon brown sugar and salt, if needed. These measurements are for each cup of mashed potato. Add some butter or margarine, 1 teaspoon to each cup of potato is enough, unless you have more to spare.

Stuff the orange skins with the mashed potatoes. This may be done ahead of time. Arrange them in a pan. Bake in the oven ½ hour or until hot through. Plan to have them with some meat that is also in the oven.

Pork Roast

You can have a brown, crusty, fragrant roast of pork without spending much time in the kitchen. The long time needed for pork roast can be distributed according to your schedule. The morning can be used to advantage if you are having the roast for dinner at night. Or if it is for dinner at noon, start it the night before. Allow the roast to bake until almost done. Keep the last hour of baking for the hour before the meal.

Wipe a pork loin roast weighing about 5 pounds with a damp cloth and rub it with a mixture of 2 tablespoons of flour, 3 tablespoons salt, ¼ teaspoon pepper. Place it in an uncovered roaster or pan, with the fat side up. Sear it in a hot oven of 475 degrees for half an hour. Turn the heat down to 325 degrees and roast 1½ hours longer. If you have any fruit juice on hand, orange, apple or pineapple, baste the roast with this now and then.

Turn off the heat and allow the roast to stand in the pan until an hour before you wish to serve it. If you find much fat in the pan, skim it off. Peeled potatoes may be arranged around the roast. Finish roasting in a hot oven, 450 to 475 degrees, for 1 hour. If the potatoes are not done, more time will not bother the pork roast.

If you used fruit juice, the gravy will be delectable. Thicken with a little flour and water and bring to a good boil.

A roast of this size will serve a family of 6 with some leftover to serve cold with hot potato salad. Here is the recipe for it.

6 cups of diced, cold, cooked potatoes, ½ cup of chopped celery, ½ cup chopped green onion, 1 cup chopped dill pickle, 1 teaspoon celery seed, 1 cup of mayonnaise, ⅓ cup vinegar, 1 teaspoon dry mustard, 1 teaspoon sugar, 1 teaspoon salt. Combine potatoes, celery, onion, pickle and celery seed. Mix other ingredients and add to potatoes.

Heat in a double boiler for 30 minutes. This is amazingly good and the best part is that the salad can be made any time, and heated up later. It is good with any cold meat. If you have some salad leftover for the next day, try it cold. It has a mellow flavor. Everybody likes potato salad, so don't hesitate to try this on your family. This amount will serve 6 to 8 people.

Fresh Ham Roasted

IF YOU are having guests for a week end and you want to be out with the gang having fun skiing or skating, make your plans a few days before and write them all out so you don't have to crack your brains trying to remember this and that.

Buy a fresh ham and soak it for 24 hours in a marinade consisting of dry white wine, sliced onions, a bay leaf, some parsley and celery leaves. A clove of garlic is advised. Turn the ham every now and then so it is equally treated on all sides.

Figure the time it will take to roast your ham, 30 minutes to a pound, so be sure to remember how much the butcher said it weighed. Remove the ham from the marinade and roast it in an oven 300 degrees, the length of time you figured it needs. Baste now and then with the marinade. When it is nearly done, remove the outer skin and sprinkle the ham with bread crumbs and put it in the oven to brown.

You may get as far as removing the skin from the ham. Then forget it for a few hours if you wish. It will stay a little warm in the oven with the heat turned off. About half an hour before dinner, sprinkle it with crumbs and allow it to brown and get hot through while you have a cocktail with your guests. Maybe you have scalloped potatoes that baked while the ham was going full tilt. They also come to bubbling heat in this last half hour.

Remove the handsome roast to a hot platter and boil the remaining marinade (if you had any leftover after a few bastings) with the gravy in the pan. A few minutes' boiling will do. Serve this sauce with the ham.

The size of the ham determines how many people can be served. Just hope you have some leftover for sandwiches to serve with a green salad.

Slice of Ham Baked

THE ever-popular inch-thick slice of ham takes on an added flavor when covered with ½ cup of maple syrup, ½ cup of water and 1 teaspoon of vinegar. Use a baking dish big enough to accommodate 4 peeled potatoes, sliced or cut in quarters, or sweet potatoes may be substituted. 4 apples cored and stuffed with raisins join the potatoes and ham. Orange marmalade makes a nice stuffing for the apples if you have it.

This casserole or baking dish can be arranged and put aside until an hour before dinner time. Bake it at 350 degrees for an hour. This will serve 4.

Ham with Apricots

A SLICE of ham 3 inches thick and weighing about 3 pounds takes nicely to this treatment, with a delectable result.

Cover the slice with the juice from a large can of apricots and bake it at 300 degrees for 1 hour. Then place the apricot halves on the ham. Mix 1 teaspoon of ground cloves and 1 teaspoon of dry mustard with 2 tablespoons of brown sugar. Sprinkle this over the ham and apricots and continue baking for 20 minutes more.

Several vegetables, including potatoes, may be baked at the same time. 6 persons can be bountifully fed and perhaps a little ham will be leftover for lunch the next day. Every scrap of ham can be used. Even a half cup of ground ham will pep up an omelet.

Baked Ham and Potatoes

PLACE a slice of raw ham 1 inch thick, weighing at least a pound, in a baking dish. Slice thinly 4 medium potatoes over the ham, sprinkling lightly with salt and pepper. Fill the dish with enough milk to cover potatoes. Bake 1 hour in an oven 350 degrees. Enough for 4.

Follow with some favorite dessert and coffee. Spiced Apple Snow is perfect.

Cheese and Ham Casserole

THIS is a Wisconsin stand-by. Get it ready in the morning or even the night before.

You need 2 cups of ground ham, either raw or cooked. Mix it with ½ pound of Wisconsin American cheese cut into tiny bits and ½ a green pepper also cut fine; minced is even better.

Cook 2 6-ounce packages of fine noodles according to directions on the package; drain well. Mix lightly into the ham and cheese. Add 1 cup of sliced mushrooms and 1 can of condensed tomato soup.

Bake in a greased casserole for 1 hour in an oven heated to 350 degrees. Serves 6 or 8 people.

Gracie's Ham and Rice Dinner

WOMEN who paint get hungry after toting easels and canvas and paint boxes over the landscape. Puttering in the kitchen does not appeal after a hard day's work. Gracie often prepares this dish in the morning and keeps it in the refrigerator until an hour before dinner. It is popular with her friends who enjoy a cocktail and an inspection of the latest canvas while the oven takes care of the dinner.

Grease a good-sized casserole or baking dish and put in a layer of cooked rice. You need 3 or 4 cups of cooked rice for the entire dish. The layers are about 2 inches deep. Between the layers distribute 1 pound of boiled or tenderized ham cut in bite-sized chunks. Over this ensemble pour 1 large can of tomatoes.

Top with as much diced cheese as you like, and bake in a slow oven not over 350 degrees for 1 hour. This amount will serve 5 or 6.

Gracie bolsters up the meal with a crusty loaf of French or Italian bread freshened a few minutes in the oven, and a large bowl of salad, mostly greens.

Ham Mousse

So MANY men scorn a dish made with gelatin, but this mousse amply fortified with ham seems to please them. It is a good supper dish for hot weather. Of course there is no objection to serving it during the other seasons of the year.

If you have the time to haul out the old-fashioned chopping bowl, you will have a better result. But few of us do that nowdays. We use the grinder. The recipe calls for 3 cups of chopped, cold, lean cooked ham. A coarse grinder turns out bits of ham not too fine.

Chop 2 small stalks of celery and 1 green pepper very fine. A sharp paring knife will do it. Chop ½ cup of capers, 2 tablespoons dill pickle and the same of parsley. Mix with the ham and add 2 teaspoons of Worcestershire sauce and 2 tablespoons of grated onion.

Soak 2 tablespoons of plain gelatin in 3 tablespoons of cold water. When it is dissolved, add it to ¾ cup of hot meat stock. If you have no meat stock on hand, use bouillon cubes, either beef or chicken melted in hot water. Pour in ¼ cup of sherry. Taste and add as much salt and pepper as you think advisable. Blend it into the ham mixture.

Fold in 1¾ cups of heavy cream, whipped. You may use undiluted, chilled evaporated milk, whipped stiff. Sprinkle with a few grains of curry powder.

Dip the mold you plan to use, in cold water. Pour in the mixture gently and chill in the refrigerator until stiff. Overnight is best, although if prepared in the morning for an evening meal, it will be stiff. You can hurry it by turning the cold control on the refrigerator to a more frigid temperature.

Garnish the mold as your fancy directs. It is very handsome and colorful, and will serve 8 to 10 people.

Bologna Rolls

DON'T snicker, they are awfully good. Easy to make beforehand, all ready to pop into the oven. 4 pancakes made from Bisquick if they are large ones, will do for 4 people. Directions are given on the package. Make them thin by using a little more liquid than the recipe calls for. Thin slices of bologna sausage, ¼ of a pound for 4 pancakes, are laid on the cakes and sprinkled with either grated Parmesan cheese or grated American cheese. Roll the pancakes and lay in a casserole. Pour a rich cream sauce over them. 2 cups of sauce is made by melting 3 tablespoons of butter or margarine in a saucepan with 4 tablespoons of flour added and stirred smooth. Gradually add the milk and cook until thick. Add minced parsley and chives for color.

Heat until bubbling hot in a moderate oven. That is 350 degrees, and the time will be about 20 minutes.

Polenta with Sausages

Into 6 cups of boiling salted water, gradually stir in 1½ cups of cornmeal. Cook over slow heat, stirring often. Some cooks stir and cook this mush for 40 minutes. I put it in the double boiler after 10 minutes of boiling and let it cook half an hour with only a stir now and then. Pour on a platter to the depth of ½ inch. Cool.

Cook ½ pound of pork sausages.

Cut cold mush into inch squares and sausages in slices. Place in layers in buttered casserole. Sprinkle with Parmesan cheese. Add the sauce and bake ½ hour in 350 degree oven. Just before serving, add 1 cup of white wine, heat through and serve. Enough for 4.

Sauce: 1 tablespoon olive oil, in saucepan; stir in 1 tablespoon of flour, 1 teaspoon beef extract dissolved in hot water, or 1 beef cube in ½ cup hot water. Cook until smooth, a few minutes. Add 2 pounds of peeled tomatoes, cut up, 2 minced white onions, bit of a bay leaf, pinch of origanum or thyme, 2 cloves, ½ cup chopped parsley. Simmer slowly until it thickens. Remove and add 1 tablespoon of butter.

This dish can be assembled in the morning and baked for half an hour before dinner time. The white wine is optional but don't

leave it out if you can help it, for it bestows a final blessing on the
Polenta.

Roast Veal

THE veal I roasted in this fashion was 4 ribs wide, it weighed 2
pounds. Make a marinade of 1 small onion minced, 1 teaspoon
celery flakes or chopped leaves, a pinch of thyme, juice of half a
lemon and ¼ cup of sherry. Mix and stuff into a fold in the meat.
If you can't find a fold or pocket, make one with a sharp knife.
Leave the roast in a cool place long enough for the marinade to
season the meat. A few hours will suffice.

Then dredge the roast with flour, a little salt and pepper. Roast
it in an oven 350 degrees for 2½ hours. The slow roasting does
away with basting and frequent peeps in the oven to see how
things are going.

Place the roast, when done, on a hot platter and make a gravy
in the pan, adding ½ teaspoon of Worcestershire or A1 sauce.

Of course, the wise cook will have potatoes baking and apples
perhaps touched up with cinnamon, rum and sugar.

If the potatoes are started early enough they can be stuffed and
put back to heat fifteen minutes before the roast is done. To stuff
baked potatoes, cut off one side, put the scooped-out potato
through a ricer or mash using rich milk, salt and pepper. Put back
in the shells and dot with butter.

Plum jam is a "must" with roast veal. This small roast managed
to serve 4 people—just managed.

Veal Pot Roast with Vegetables

UTILITY cuts of meat that are cheap and rather bony should be
treated with imagination. Veal offers a number of delicious dishes.

Flour a 2½ or 3-pound piece of veal. Brown it in bacon fat in an iron pot known as a Dutch Oven. Put in a snippet of garlic. Turn the meat to brown on all sides. Add 1 cup of water, the juice of ½ a lemon, 1 teaspoon salt and ¼ teaspoon pepper, ¼ teaspoon cinnamon, 1 tablespoon sugar and 4 tomatoes cut up. Canned tomatoes may be used. Cover and simmer over low heat for an hour and a half or until the meat is very tender when pierced with a fork. If this is done during the morning, the heat may be turned off. An hour before dinner, put in 4 peeled potatoes, tucking them around the meat. Add a pound of string beans left whole, except to snip off the ends and string them if they need it. Cover and cook over a low flame for an hour. Remove the meat and vegetables to a serving dish. Thicken the gravy with 3 tablespoons of flour blended with ½ cup of water. Cook and stir the gravy for a few minutes, then give it a drop or two of A1 sauce or Worcestershire and 3 tablespoons of Burgundy. The wine is optional.

To my mind there is nothing so perfect with the delicate blandness of veal as an accompanying dish of plum jam. This will serve 4 very bountifully.

Veal Chops Stifled in Onions

THIS is something to smack your lips over. It is a way of preparing veal that men like.

Brown in hot fat as many veal chops as are needed for the family. Bacon fat is best for the browning and for the onions. Fry lots of onions cut in slices. They have a way of shrinking after cooking, so cut up more than you think you need. By the way, peeling onions without tears is easy. Fill a large pan with water and peel the onions under water.

Combine the onions and chops and add enough hot water to cover. The juice of ½ a lemon will be enough for 4 chops. Add with 1 teaspoon of salt and ½ teaspoon of pepper and 1 teaspoon of paprika. Cover and cook over low heat for 1 hour.

There should be plenty of liquid for a gravy if the heat has been kept low, low enough and still hot enough to keep up a gentle simmering during the hour.

Thicken the gravy with flour and water mixed smooth. For 4 chops use 3 tablespoons of flour and ½ cup water. If this dish is prepared in the morning, it can be heated just before dinner. The flavors will have had a chance to blend and develop. Now comes the real gourmet touch. Add some sour cream before serving, as much as you like up to 1 cup for 4 or 5 chops. Serve on a platter with the onions draped over the chops. If you want to be daring, keep the sour cream until now and put it in dabs here and there on top of the onions. Looks pretty that way.

Veal Loaf

1½ POUNDS of ground veal, ½ pound of ground, lean salt pork. Mix with ½ cup of fine, dry bread crumbs or 3 tablespoons of rolled cracker crumbs. Mix in a large bowl and add ½ cup of chopped celery, ¼ cup chopped parsley, 2 tablespoons lemon juice, 2 eggs slightly beaten, 1 cup canned tomatoes or fresh, skinned, chopped tomatoes, ¼ teaspoon salt, ½ teaspoon pepper, ¼ teaspoon nutmeg.

Pack into a greased loaf pan and bake 1 hour in a moderate oven, 350 degrees. You can dice 2 slices of bacon and sprinkle it over the top before baking, but the loaf is good without it. This will serve 6.

Marjorie's Easy Corn Pudding

GREASE a baking dish with bacon fat. Empty a can of cream-style corn into the dish. Break in 2 eggs and stir with a fork until mixed. Pour in 1 cup of milk while stirring. Add 1 tablespoon of sugar,

½ teaspoon of salt and sprinkle the top with dry bread crumbs and paprika. Sometimes Marjorie chips half a green pepper into the dish. Put the dish in a pan of hot water and bake 1 hour at the same time the veal loaf is in the oven. Very simple and always perfect.

My pet Graham Icebox Pudding is made a day ahead.

Veal Tenderloin

CUT the slice of veal in bite-sized pieces. Brown them lightly in hot fat. Then put them in a casserole and cover with hot water, 2 onions sliced, 1 teaspoon of salt and ½ teaspoon of pepper. Bake this for an hour in an oven of 350 degrees. Melinna serves this with tomato sauce or Spanish Omelet sauce, either sauce bought canned.

This can all be cooked in the morning and heated to the simmering point in a few minutes just before dinner time.

Veal Terrapin

EVERY cook welcomes leftover veal. It is so adaptable. Three people feast royally on 1 cup of cold veal cut in slivers. 1 cup of gravy, 1 cup of milk, a pinch of mace, paprika, about 1 teaspoon to give color and flavor. Cook over a gentle flame. If the sauce is not thick enough mix 1 tablespoon of flour with a little cold milk and stir into the sauce and continue cooking. The sieved yolk of a hard-boiled egg and the white cut in slivers, are now added. Put in the veal, just before it is hot, add 1 tablespoon of sherry, bring to a good heat and serve at once.

This recipe can be varied by substituting 1 teaspoon curry powder or 1 teaspoon chili powder for the sherry. Only, then it is not Veal Terrapin, it is Veal Curry or Veal Chili.

Chili Veal

LEFTOVER veal makes this spicy stew that calls for the addition of a package of wide noodles boiled according to directions on the box.

I make a sauce starting with bacon fat in which a large onion and 2 medium-sized green peppers are cooked until tender. Mince them first of course. Then add 3 large tomatoes, also cut up, but not so finely.

Season with 1 teaspoon salt, 1 teaspoon chili powder. Cook gently for 15 or 20 minutes. Add 2 cups of leftover gravy or extend the gravy if you haven't enough, with a bouillon cube dissolved in hot water.

Tomato juice may be used if you have opened a can of tomatoes to substitute for fresh ones. Allow this sauce to cook slowly a few more minutes to blend the flavors.

I used veal from a pot roast that had been pointed up with Burgundy and the flavor was tantalizing. Between 3 and 4 cups of leftover veal cut into small pieces will serve 4 people. If you allow the stew to simmer after the meat has been added, the flavors ripen and it needs only a few minutes to heat it up before dinner.

Serve it with the boiled noodles.

The perfect dessert is Honey and Sherry on Fruit.

Stuffed Pancakes

ALL recipes for thin pancakes vary somewhat. The best pancakes I ever had were prepared by Tony Perrett in the morning and brought forth at a buffet dinner with no visible effort on her part. They were filled with a chopped mixture of cold roast veal and a few vegetables, carrots, peas and string beans. On the same plate was some applesauce with plump raisins stewed in the sauce. A peach-half with a cooked prune in the hollow completed the color effect.

Tony's rule is 1 tablespoon of flour to 1 egg and enough milk to make a thin batter. 6 eggs beaten with 6 tablespoons of flour and ½ teaspoon of salt with enough milk added to make a thin batter will produce 14 pancakes cooked in an 8-inch skillet. She always uses lard in the pan to grease it.

I have used 5 eggs and 10 tablespoons of flour, ½ teaspoon of salt and 1⅔ cups of milk to make 8 pancakes. Mix until smooth. Place 1 teaspoon of Wesson oil in the skillet. When it is hot, pour in enough batter to cover the pan as you tilt the pan to make the batter spread evenly. Brown over medium heat. If they are very thin they will cook through and not need to be turned. The browned side should be nicely freckled. If you did not turn the pancake use the brown side for the outside.

The filling can be as varied as your imagination suggests. Chopped cold roast, chicken, fish, lobster or shrimp, moistened with leftover gravy or a rich white sauce, are good. Spread in the center of each cake and roll up. Place them close together in a shallow baking dish.

Heat in an oven 350 degrees for 20 minutes before serving. Allow 2 pancakes for each person.

The pancakes may be filled with drained, hot, buttered canned fruit, and sweetened a little more with brown sugar. Creamed vegetables, if you have an interesting combination, make a meatless meal.

Veal Patties

THIS is one of my stand-bys. Usually I plan to have stuffed potatoes and some vegetable that goes in the oven too, when I have the Veal Patties.

You can change the seasonings to suit your fancy, as veal is so mild and takes so profitably to delicate hints of herbs and the various salts. 1 teaspoon celery salt, a pinch of sage, ½ teaspoon nutmeg, ¼ teaspoon cinnamon or grated lemon rind are some suggestions.

Have 2 pounds of ground veal and mix it with 1 cup of soft bread crumbs, 2 well-beaten eggs, and ½ cup of milk. Evaporated milk is very good in this recipe. You need some fat—3 tablespoons of melted butter or margarine and salt and pepper, 2 teaspoons of salt and ¼ teaspoon of pepper. I like to use 2 tablespoons of lemon juice and some grated rind and 1 teaspoon of celery salt. I have tossed in ½ cup of chopped raisins when I felt experimental. They are really quite an addition.

Form the mixture into 8 balls. Do not flatten them out. Keep them rather round and encircle each ball with a strip of bacon. Secure the bacon with a toothpick. In each ball insert a bit of bay leaf.

Keep the balls in the refrigerator, covered of course, until 1 hour before dinner. Bake them for 1 hour in an oven heated to 350 degrees. If you have time, baste them once or twice with the fat in the pan. Each ball should be large enough for one serving. But veal has a way of shrinking, so perhaps you had better plan this dinner for 5 or 6 people.

Leg of Lamb Swedish Style

MARJORIE BENÉT and I worked out this marvelous roast lamb in a perfectly satisfactory manner. No longer do we hang around the kitchen basting and peering into the oven.

This is how. Wipe a 5 or 5½-pound leg of lamb with a damp cloth. Jab a sharp, pointed knife into the surface and insert little slivers of garlic. 1 clove of garlic sliced is plenty. Rub the meat with 1 tablespoon of salt, 1 teaspoon dry mustard. Place the roast in the oven heated to 350 degrees.

The time needed for roasting is 2½ to 3 hours. You can start the roast in the morning, and not quite finish it. The last hour of roasting can be done just before dinner time at night. Or, if you wish, the entire time can be used. Baste when half done, with 1 cup of strong coffee sweetened with 2 teaspoons of sugar and amplified with 2 teaspoons of cream, 1 pony of brandy and a very little water.

Turn the roast and baste it all over. Now forget it. If you plan to finish the roasting period later on, allow an hour for it. Most roasts can be partly roasted and then left for the finishing hour later on.

At the end of 3 hours' roasting, whether done in one fell swoop or not, you should have some pan juice as a starter for the gravy.

Stir in 5 tablespoons of flour until smooth, add ¾ cup of cream and 2 tablespoons of currant jelly. Cook until bubbling. The gravy is divine and the meat is seasoned so deliciously and is so fragrant that faces will beam when it is sliced, and sighs of regret to think no more can possibly be eaten will disturb the after-dinner torpor.

Lamb Stew

THIS will please the man of the house, especially if he is the kind who is always talking about the stews his mother used to make.

Buy 2 pounds of lean lamb meat for stew and cut it into small pieces. Brown on all sides in 1 teaspoon of fat. Bacon is good. Use a large, heavy frying pan or Dutch Oven type of pot. Add 4 cups of hot water, 1 teaspoon salt, ¼ teaspoon pepper, a pinch of thyme and a pinch of marjoram. Toss in 2 celery tops and 1 carrot. Cook over very low heat for 2 hours. Now cool and chill long enough to bring all the fat to the top. Skim it off, every bit, because this eliminates all muttony flavor.

An hour before dinner, reheat to boiling and add 1 cup of cubed raw potatoes, 1 cup diced carrots, 1 cup diced celery, 1 cup green beans or any other green vegetable and 4 peeled onions. At the end of the hour the vegetables should be tender and the meat likewise. Thicken with 2 tablespoons of flour stirred into ½ cup of water. If you think there isn't enough liquid to make plenty of gravy, eke it out with hot water fortified with a chicken or beef bouillon cube.

This will feed a family of 6. Of course there is no reason you should not have dumplings with the stew. Use the recipe on a package of Bisquick.

Collops

LAMB kidneys are combined with chopped beef. Wash 6 lamb kidneys, split and remove skin and fat. Soak in cold salted water for 1 hour. Drain and slice thin.

Fry 1 medium-sized chopped onion in 2 tablespoons of fat for 5 minutes. Add 1 pound of chopped beef and the kidneys. Fry quickly until browned. Stir in 1 tablespoon of flour, add 1 cup of water gradually, bring to a boil stirring constantly. Add 1 teaspoon beef extract and 1 tablespoon catsup, ½ teaspoon celery salt, 1 teaspoon salt and ⅛ teaspoon pepper. Simmer for 20 minutes.

If you plan to take the afternoon off, do this in the morning and let the whole thing slide off your conscience until a few minutes before dinner time. Bring to a bubbling boil and serve at once. 6 people partial to lamb kidneys will bless you.

Chicken Creole

THIS is something to rave about. Your imagination can vary the seasonings, especially with herbs. The tomatoes may be stewed with a sprig of basil or a bay leaf or few tarragon leaves. A pinch of saffron or filé powder will give it a real southern touch.

First, combine 3 cups of diced cooked chicken with 1½ cups of cold boiled rice. Mix into this 2 cups of stewed tomatoes, either canned or fresh. Cook over a low flame for 10 or 12 minutes. Toss in 3 stalks of celery, 2 good-sized onions and 1 large sweet green pepper, all cut very fine. Cook over a low flame 10 minutes. Add ½ teaspoon salt and ⅛ teaspoon pepper and a few grains of nutmeg.

Grease a baking dish and pour the mixture into it and liberally cover the top with buttered bread crumbs. Bake for 1 hour in an oven heated to 350 degrees. If the top is getting too brown, lay a tin pie plate or cover over the dish. 6 can be amply served with this amount.

Of course this is one of those dishes that can be waiting in the refrigerator all day or overnight. Before baking, in that case, allow the dish to come to room temperature and be sure to have the dish covered while it is in the refrigerator. If you have been stewing a tough old fowl, keep the water in which it cooks simmering ever so gently. The long, slow cooking turns the fowl into tender, juicy meat.

Chicken Forshmak

THIS is a heavenly way to use up leftovers. Have 1 cup of cubed cold chicken, ½ cup of cubed cooked ham, ¾ cup of cubed cold potatoes.

Fry 1 finely minced onion in 2 tablespoons butter or margarine. Remove onions from pan, leaving as much butter in pan as possible. In this butter fry ½ pound of sliced mushrooms for 10 minutes or until brown. Add the onions to the mushrooms, toss in the chicken, ham and potatoes. Pour in 1 cup of cream or top milk or evaporated milk, and enough hot water to show through the mixture. Season with 1 teaspoon salt and ⅛ teaspoon of pepper. Simmer very gently until the mixture is smooth and slightly moist. Pour it into a buttered casserole, sprinkle with ⅓ cup of grated cheese and bake 25 minutes in an oven heated to 350 degrees. The top should be brown.

This dish may be prepared and left ready for the final baking, allowing ½ an hour for the oven to get hot. It will serve 4 or 6.

If I can find out from Irina what Forshmak means I will tell you. Otherwise, take my word for it, it is Russian.

Melinna's Chicken

BOIL a 5 or 6-pound chicken in salted water to cover. When tender, allow it to cool in the broth. Remove meat from bones in quite large pieces and place in the center of a round or oval serving dish. If you plan to serve this later in the day, be sure the dish is heatproof so it can go into the oven.

Have the white meat on top. Arrange 2 cups of boiled rice around the edge of the dish. With the broth, make 1½ pints of gravy by thickening it with 3 tablespoons of flour moistened with cold water and beaten smooth. Cook until thick. In this gravy Melinna may put in some canned mushrooms, tomatoes or cooked peas. She seasons it with celery salt and paprika.

Half of the gravy is poured over the chicken and the other half is served in a gravy boat. Boiled onions are arranged in clusters at each end of the oval dish, or if the dish is round, they may be in a wreath studding the rice ring. Pour browned butter or margarine over the onions.

If this has been prepared in the morning, allow time to bring it all to a good steaming heat. Half an hour in a moderate oven should do it.

6 are at the dinner table for this recipe.

Norwegian Chicken with Caraway Seed

DON'T turn the page and say, "Not for me, caraway seeds always get wedged between my teeth." If they do, see your dentist twice a year. Soon it will be three times a year and then four times a year. Anyway, if the seeds are pounded in a bit of cloth with a hammer, you have the tantalizing flavor and no hard seeds.

Have a fowl cut up. The toughest old bird responds to this treatment. Wipe the pieces with a damp cloth. Flour them well, season with salt and pepper. Brown in a frying pan deep enough and wide enough to accommodate them without shoving. A Dutch Oven does nicely if you have one.

Add 2 tablespoons of caraway seeds, some herbs you may fancy, but they are optional. Pour in ½ cup of hot water and 1 cup of sour cream. Cover closely and let the pan simmer gently 1½ hours. Test the meat with a fork to see if it is tender. You may bake this in a slow oven 300 degrees, also having the pan covered. Allow ½ an hour for the final cooking.

At this point you may remove the chicken from the heat and let it stand until ½ an hour before dinner. Then bring it to a good heat and pour in 1 cup of sour cream. Serve at once. There should have been enough flour on the chicken when it was being browned so that the gravy in the pan does not need to be thickened. The sour cream used is the kind you order from the milkman. It is not rancid, but very delicate in flavor. Many people like it on fresh fruit better than sweet cream.

A fowl weighing 5 pounds serves 5 or 6 people.

Roast Chicken

BUY a roasting chicken weighing 4 or 5 pounds. Be sure to remove the lungs. The butcher seldom does it. Wipe out the inside with a damp cloth. Some cooks never rinse the inside of a chicken, but I do. Then I wipe it with a dry cloth and sprinkle a little salt inside.

A prepared stuffing is easy but if you add a minced onion and a little finely chopped celery, cooked till soft in bacon fat, you get a better flavor. If you are an herb addict, put in a tiny pinch of your favorite herb. Stuff the chicken, pin the opening with the metal skewers used for this purpose, or sew it up in the old-fashioned way with a darning needle and string. Tie the legs together.

Rub the bird with fat, sprinkle with salt, pepper and flour. Some cooks place a strip of bacon or salt pork over the breast bone. Make a slit lengthwise in the strip so it will slip over the breast bone and stay in place. Cover the roaster and bake 1½ hours in an oven between 300 and 350 degrees. Turn off the heat and forget the chicken until half an hour before dinner. Take off the cover and finish roasting in an oven set at 400 degrees. Baste once. The chicken should be browned and there should be enough fat and browned flour in the pan to make a good gravy.

If you are doubtful about that, dissolve a chicken bouillon cube in a cup of hot water. Take the chicken from the roaster, and pour in the bouillon, thicken with flour and water, cook and stir until smooth. If you like a dark gravy, add a few drops of Gravy Master or Kitchen Bouquet. Read the directions on the bottle so you don't use more than is recommended.

This method makes it possible to have a roast chicken for dinner in very little time. Start it in the morning and finish it just before dinner time. If you want this for noon dinner, the preliminary cooking can be done the night before. This means, however, that you must keep the bird cool and allow for time to bring it to room temperature before the final roasting.

Creamed Chicken in a Ring of Rice

THIS is one of those festive-appearing dishes that makes an entrance with no fussing beforehand.

The rice is boiled first. Wash 1 cup of rice and sprinkle it into 2 quarts of boiling salted water. Allow it to boil without stirring for 25 minutes. Drain and rinse the rice. Season it with ½ teaspoon of nutmeg or ½ teaspoon celery salt or ½ teaspoon curry powder. Arrange the rice in a well-buttered ring mold not over 7 inches in diameter. Dot generously with butter or margarine, using ¼ of a cup of either. 20 minutes before serving time place the ring in a pan of hot water and bake it in an oven heated to 350 degrees. Run a knife around the sides of the mold and gently turn it onto a large round plate.

I lay the plate over the mold and turn it upside down. Easy does it.

Any time during the day prepare a rich sauce by melting 2 tablespoons butter, margarine or chicken fat. Stir in 2 tablespoons of flour. Blend well. Gradually add 1½ cups of liquid, cream and part chicken broth, or rich milk. Use your imagination and be daring with the liquids and seasonings. It is conventional to use ¼ teaspoon salt and ⅛ teaspoon paprika or pepper. But you may add other flavorings. 2 tablespoons of sherry is good, stirred in at the last minute.

While the rice ring is heating in the oven, bring the sauce to a good heat in the top of the double boiler. Add 2 cups of cut-up chicken. You may use mushrooms, shrimp, cooked leftover fish. Finnan haddie is good, too. Even the plebeian salt codfish, freshened according to directions on the package, is tasty in a rice ring.

Tinned lobster or salmon look very handsome in a rice ring. Trim it all with chopped parsley and chives if you have them. This amount will serve 6.

Chicken à la Indue

HAVE the butcher cut up a nice fowl into serving pieces. Sprinkle the chicken with flour, salt and pepper, and brown it well in 4 tablespoons of fat. Turn each piece to get an even color all over.

While this is going on, get out the grinder and use the finest blade. Grind 1 large onion, 1 teaspoon of coriander seeds, ½ teaspoon caraway seeds. This makes a kind of paste. Mix into it ¼ teaspoon of tumeric.

When the chicken has browned nicely, spread this paste over each piece. Put enough water in the frying pan to make about an inch of liquid in the pan. Cover closely and simmer over a very low flame until tender. You may have to add more water if it seems to cook away.

The length of time needed depends on the tenderness of the chicken. I do this in the morning and allow the flavors to blend and ripen during the rest of the day. Bring it to bubbling heat just before dinner time. Make a gravy with the liquid left in the pan. If there is not enough, use hot water with a chicken bouillon cube dissolved in it.

The coriander and caraway seeds give a delicate flavor to the chicken that is indescribable. It is the flavor a Hindu cook gets, and of course the Hindu cook serves dry, flaky, boiled rice that has been cooked in water with a little onion minced in it. The onion is strained from the water before the rice is added.

The perfect dessert is a Fruit Salad with a West Indian dressing. It is delicious and entirely different from other dressings.

Becky's Sunday Dinner

A BUSINESS woman who likes Sunday without a maid has a 4-pound chicken cooked on Saturday. The meat is removed from the bones, cut up and stored in the refrigerator. A white sauce is also tucked into the refrigerator. It is made by melting in a saucepan, 3 tablespoons of butter or margarine. Blend in 5 tablespoons of flour, 1 teaspoon salt and 3 cups of rich milk. Cook until smooth.

There is also ½ pound of cheese, grated and wrapped in wax paper.

All that Becky has to do on this maidless Sunday is to boil 1½ packages of macaroni according to directions on the box.

In a large baking dish she arranges three layers of chicken, the drained macaroni and the white sauce with some cheese between each layer. Enough cheese should be on the top to allow for a nice crust. This is baked ¾ of an hour in an oven set at 350 degrees. You may allow an hour if you wish. The time doesn't seem to matter. It always comes out bubbly and brown and serves 6. Guests having cocktails on the terrace are sometimes a bit reluctant to be hurried in to dinner.

Chicken Loaf

IF YOU have only 1 cup of cooked chopped chicken leftover, don't despair. Perhaps you have 2 cups of the broth that the fowl was cooked in. If not, use 2 or 3 chicken bouillon cubes in 2 cups of hot water. Bring to a boil and add ½ cup of finely chopped celery, a sprig of tarragon and stir in ½ cup of hominy grits. Boil and stir until thick. This can be done in the top of the double boiler if you haven't time to stand and stir the mush.

Toss in the chopped chicken, ¼ cup of broken walnut meats, 1 teaspoon of paprika, ¼ cup of dry bread crumbs. Beat two eggs slightly with ½ cup of milk.

If you are doing this in the morning, let it remain in the mixing bowl. Line a bread pan with heavy waxed paper an hour and a half before dinner time. This loaf should bake slowly for an hour or a little longer. Heat the oven to 350 degrees. Pour the mixture into the bread pan. Set this pan in a larger pan with an inch of hot water in it. Bake until dinner time.

A can of mushroom soup, undiluted, makes a good sauce to pour over each serving. A dehydrated mushroom sauce made according to directions on the package can be made hours beforehand and heated at the last moment. This loaf is very delicate and must be turned out on a platter with care. It will serve 4.

Chicken Pot Pie

THIS is a handsome dish to haul out of the refrigerator and pop into the oven.

Start out this way. Have 3 cups of diced leftover chicken and 3 potatoes peeled and sliced. Place them in alternate layers in a greased casserole or deep pie plate.

Now, brown 1 teaspoon of minced onion in 2 tablespoons of chicken fat. Stir in ¼ cup of flour and gradually add 2 cups of chicken stock. If lacking 2 cups, make up the measure by melting chicken bouillon cubes in hot water, 1 cube to a cup. Cook gently until smooth. Season with 1 teaspoon salt, ¼ teaspoon pepper and a little chopped parsley or chervil. Pour this sauce over the chicken and potatoes.

Make up half a recipe of pie dough, cut it in strips and place them in a crisscross design on top of the chicken and potatoes.

If you keep this in the refrigerator, allow it to come to room temperature before baking 1 hour in an oven heated to 350 degrees. This will serve 6.

Chicken à la Cacciatoria

THIS is a wonderful company dish and it is achieved with a minimum of effort. All the recipes I have encountered called for too much time to be spent in cooking before dinner. I am proud of my experiment.

The day before the dinner party, boil a 5-pound fowl in salted water to cover. Put in a bit of bay leaf. Simmer until tender. Allow to cool in broth. Remove flesh from bones and keep in rather large pieces. Store in the refrigerator.

Put 3 tablespoons of olive oil in a saucepan, 2 green peppers and 2 onions cut up and a clove of garlic—more than a clove if you are partial to garlic. Cook gently until the vegetables are soft. Add 1 quart of canned tomatoes, 1 can of tomato paste, 1 teaspoon salt and ⅛ teaspoon of pepper, 2 fresh basil leaves or a whiff of dried basil, a pinch of dried marjoram, a few celery flakes and 2 teaspoons of paprika. Cook slowly for 20 minutes, stirring it now and then.

During the morning of the day when you are having guests, boil a package of wide noodles until tender, drain and rinse with cold water. The serving dish must be of some ware that can go in the oven. I have a large oval earthenware dish. The noodles are arranged around the edge like a wreath of ivory-tinted ribbons. The chicken is placed in the center and the sauce is ladled over the entire dish. Forget it until 30 minutes before dinner time. Then heat it in an oven set at 350 degrees.

It is a handsome affair with a sprinkle of vivid parsley to set it off. This experiment graced a celebration dinner for a new book of poems by Bill. 4 ate as much as they could. 6 might have been served generously.

Chicken Chinoise

IF YOU are tired of Chicken à la King, try this recipe. It is very delicious and pleases folks a lot.

First, have 3 cups of cooked diced chicken on hand.

In a good-sized saucepan cook 1 cup of drained crushed pineapple in 4 tablespoons of butter or margarine for 10 minutes, gently. Stir in 6 tablespoons of flour and blend well. Gradually add 1½ cups of chicken broth and cook with continual stirring until thick and smooth. Taste to see if it needs salt. Some broth or the water in which the chicken was cooked is salty enough. A dash of pepper and a few grains of nutmeg come next.

If you are using canned chicken you can make the stock or broth with 2 chicken bouillon cubes dissolved in 1½ cups of hot water. Taste again for flavor, as the cubes make the stock salty.

Add 3 cups of diced chicken, white meat preferred. Let it come to a rousing heat and pour it on 6 slices of toast and sprinkle with chopped almonds. Almonds give the dish its Chinese character.

If you are tired of toast, make up a double-crust recipe of pie dough. Cut 6 4-inch squares or lay a saucer on the dough and cut 6 rounds. Place them on a cooky tin and prick all over with a fork. Bake in a hot oven about 500 degrees for 10 or 12 minutes.

These are very festive and your chicken will serve 6 people.

The chicken may be prepared hours before serving and simply heated in the double boiler. It makes a nice party luncheon with everything done ahead of time.

Turkish Pilaff

SIMMER a chicken or fowl in about 2 quarts of water with 2 good-sized onions until tender. Strain off the broth and put 6 cups of it in a large saucepan with salt and pepper to taste. Be sure to taste. As soon as it comes to a rolling boil, gradually add 2 cups of washed rice. Be careful the rice does not stick to the bottom of the pan, but do not stir too much. Shake often to keep grains separated.

Shred the chicken meat into small pieces. When the rice is cooked, add the chicken, giving a few brisk stirs with a spoon. Add 1 heaping teaspoon of butter and let stand in a warm place 5 or 10 minutes before serving. This dish can be prepared a day before and reheated. It is even better reheated, and will serve 6 plentifully.

Serve with Turkish Tomatoes. This dish requires long baking, but it is unusual in flavor and can be warmed over. Open a quart can of tomatoes and take out 1 cup of the liquid. Put the tomatoes in a baking dish with ½ cup of sugar, a tiny pinch of salt and a good deal of black pepper. About ½ teaspoon suits me, but the Turks like more.

Stir well and put bits of butter over the top. Bake in a slow oven 4 or 5 hours. Cover at first to keep it from burning. It should be dark brown when done and will have shrunk about half.

The Greeks have a Chicken Pilaff done in the same manner, but with cracked wheat instead of rice. George Demetrious tells me that he buys the cracked wheat in an Armenian store. They crack it a little finer than the ordinary breakfast-food cracked wheat. The flavor of cracked wheat with the chicken, using olive oil instead of butter, is wonderfully good for Sunday dinner and whatever is leftover can be heated for supper. George and his sons like hearty meals. The boys heat the leftover Pilaff and set the table for Sunday supper. They eat large gobs of Yaurti with it. This is a cultured milk they always have on hand, saving a little to make the next batch.

Roast Turkey

MANY a cook will appreciate an easy way to have a roast turkey and still have time to enjoy the Christmas tree or Thanksgiving service.

For a turkey weighing from 10 to 16 pounds you will need about 8 cups of stuffing. First, wipe the bird clean inside and out, and rub with salt and pepper. Chill the bird thoroughly. Now make the stuffing the day before. There are several schools of thought on that matter of a stuffing. Some like it moist, some like it dry. A moist stuffing is made this way. In a large bowl have 8 cups of stale bread cubes, 1 finely minced onion, ½ cup of minced celery, ¼ cup of minced parsley, 1 teaspoon poultry seasoning, 2 teaspoons salt, ¼ teaspoon pepper, ½ cup of margarine melted in ½ cup of boiling water. Pour gradually over the bread and mix lightly. Add 1 egg beaten with ¼ cup of cold water. Mix again. Chill thoroughly.

When both bird and stuffing are chilled you may stuff the bird and put it in the refrigerator until time to roast.

I'd better give you a dry stuffing before I go further. Have 8 cups of dry bread crumbs, 1 finely minced onion, ¼ teaspoon celery seeds, 1½ teaspoons poultry seasoning, 2 teaspoons salt, ½ teaspoon pepper. Melt ¾ cup of margarine or butter and add to the crumbs, tossing lightly until well mixed. Chill and stuff later into the chilled turkey. The reason for all this chilling is because you are doing this the day before.

Now, for the roasting. Allow 25 to 30 minutes a pound for total roasting time. Heat the oven to 450 or 475 degrees. Place the turkey in the pan uncovered and brown it. Now lower the heat to 275 or 300 degrees. Pour a cup of boiling water into the pan and put on the lid tight. Bake without basting until the turkey is tender. Be sure you have figured out the time correctly. The last half hour take off the cover and you will have a crisp golden-brown crust on the turkey.

If you are wise, all sorts of vegetables can be baking at the same time.

While you are gorging on the turkey, the mince pie can be getting itself all juicy and fragrant in the hot oven.

Turkey and Sausage Pudding

THIS comes from an old-fashioned cook book. Nowdays we would call this a casserole dish. Puddings are desserts to us. But it is a tasty way to use leftover turkey when the family's appetite has begun to falter at the reappearance of the turkey.

In a buttered baking dish put a layer of turkey cut in ½-inch lengths. 1 cup is enough for this layer. Dot with butter or margarine and sprinkle with ½ cup of minced cooked sausage meat.

Put 3 or 4 chopped olives on top of this. Repeat with same ingredients, using 2 cups of chopped turkey and 1 cup of sausage meat and 6 or 8 olives in all. Over this pour 1 cup of hot turkey gravy. Cover with a crust commonly called a biscuit crust. Use Bisquick and follow directions on the package. Bake in a medium oven, 350 degrees, for ¾ of an hour.

This casserole can be prepared and kept in the refrigerator until time to bake. Allow time for the dish to come to room temperature.

This amount will serve 4 or 5 people.

Indian Curry

A FRIEND of mine who has lived in Siam says this curry tastes more like the real thing than any other he has met with since leaving Siam.

It sounds crazy to some people but it does taste good. If you can get fresh coconut milk use it instead of the almond milk.

First, put the neck and feet of a frying chicken into 2 cups of boiling water with 1 onion, 1 large carrot, 1 large stalk of celery (all cut up), ½ teaspoon salt, 6 peppercorns, 1 teaspoon beef extract. Simmer for half an hour and then strain.

The almond milk is made this way. Cover ¼ pound of almonds with boiling water. Let them stand a few minutes, but only until the skins slip off. Then put the almonds through the meat chopper. Pour over them 2 cups of scalded milk and have the dish covered and allow it to stand while the milk becomes infused with the almond flavor.

Fry the disjointed chicken in butter or margarine. Cover the pan and steam until tender over a low flame. When a fork easily pierces the leg, the rest of the chicken should be tender.

Take the meat from the bones. Make a sauce by frying 2 sliced onions in 2 tablespoons of butter or margarine until soft. Stir in at least 2 large tablespoons of curry powder, ½ teaspoon of chili powder, 2 tablespoons of flour. Stir until blended and gradually add 1 cup of the strained almond milk and the strained broth which will be about 1½ cups. Simmer in the double boiler ½ hour. Then add the chicken to the sauce and let it stand in the sauce off the fire for half an hour.

If you wish to finish this curry later in the day, it is quite all right to leave it longer.

Have ready in a cup, ⅛ teaspoon each of mace, allspice, nutmeg, cloves and cinnamon. Also add 2 teaspoons of currant jelly and 2 teaspoons of chutney and salt to taste.

Half an hour before dinner, add these seasonings to the sauce and simmer. Just before serving add the last cup of strained almond milk. Allow to heat just a few minutes and then sit down to eat it with a bowl of fluffy boiled rice that has been steaming or drying off in the oven. This will serve 4 people.

Haddock Casserole

Buy a small haddock and have it cut in 3 pieces. Take home the head and trimmings. Put in a saucepan, cover with water, add ½ teaspoon salt and I drop in a little dried or fresh dill to give flavor to the fish. Boil until the fish is white and the meat comes away from the bones easily. 15 to 20 minutes is usually enough time.

Drain and save the broth. Remove from bones and save 2 cups of flaked fish.

Make a sauce by melting 2 tablespoons of butter or margarine in a saucepan. Add 2 tablespoons of flour and stir until smooth. Gradually pour in 1 cup of the strained fish broth. Season with ½ teaspoon of salt, ⅛ teaspoon pepper, 1 teaspoon Worcestershire sauce. Cook until thick and smooth. Now add ⅓ cup of cream or top milk.

Peel and slice 3 medium-sized potatoes and slice ½ an onion. Cook together in a little salted water until tender. Drain.

Butter a baking dish and put in a layer of potatoes and onion. Then arrange 1 cup of fish over this. Put the rest of the potatoes on top. Have a dish large enough to accommodate 2 layers of each. Over all pour the sauce. Sprinkle liberally with fine bread crumbs and dot with margarine or butter. Bake for half an hour in an oven heated to 375 degrees. The top should be brown at the end of half an hour.

This casserole can be prepared and left waiting in a cool place until time to bake it. It will serve 4 or 5. Have wedges of lemon to squeeze over each serving.

Other fish may be substituted for the haddock, such as halibut, salmon, tuna or cod.

Canned peas done in Marjorie's own style are quite different. Drain juice from a can of peas. Put the liquid in a saucepan with 1 small onion finely chopped, 1 tablespoon butter or margarine, ⅛ teaspoon salt and a swift dash of pepper. Simmer this 10 minutes. Just before serving time bring it to a boil. Toss in the peas; they should be hot in a jiffy. Serve at once. A can of peas will usually serve 4 people.

Haddock Greek Style

My friend Euphemia does this on top of the stove in a covered roasting pan with medium heat. I have done it in the oven with the temperature at 350 degrees, leaving the pan uncovered and baking the fish for an hour.

Allow plenty of fish for each person. Euphemia says half a pound each. She covers the bottom of the pan with a layer of thickly sliced fresh tomatoes or drained canned tomatoes. Over this she lays a thick bed of chopped parsley. Parsley is full of iron says her uncle, George Demetrious. Now, place the fish on top of this colorful foundation.

In a bowl mix ¼ cup of olive oil with 2 tablespoons of flour, 1 teaspoon of paprika, 1 teaspoon salt and ⅛ teaspoon of pepper. Beat it well with a fork. Pour it over the fish, and proceed either to bake it or cook it on top of the stove. The stove she uses has an oil-burning unit in it and the entire top of the stove is hot as an old-fashioned coal range.

This can all be assembled during the day and kept in the refrigerator covered with wax paper until time to bake. Allow some time for the dish to come to room temperature if it is very cold.

This was originally prepared for 6 people and the haddock filet was quite large, weighed around 3 pounds.

Haddock Filet

HEREABOUTS haddock filet is simply fried as it has always been done. But I have come across one venturesome New Englander who gives a real gourmet touch to the fish.

This is quickly prepared and needs very little attention. Use a generous amount of bacon fat in a roomy frying pan. When it is hot, lay in the haddock filets cut in serving pieces. Sprinkle with celery seed, onion salt and paprika. Be generous with the seasonings. Cover and let cook for fifteen minutes. The thickness of the filet determines the time it takes to cook through. Allow more time for thick filets.

Remove the cover, pour over the fish some sour cream mixed with lemon juice. This is where your own judgment comes in. I use ½ cup of sour cream with the juice of half a lemon for 1½ pounds of fish. As soon as the cream is hot, the fish is ready for serving—with potato chips, of course. Enough for 4 people.

Filet of Sole

I HAVE two ways of preparing this delicate fish. Use either fresh or frozen filets. The first method calls for a pound of filets. Lay them in a buttered glass or earthenware baking dish. Sprinkle with salt and pepper. Go easy on the pepper. Dribble ¼ cup of cream or top milk over the fish and sprinkle with ¼ cup of fine dry bread crumbs.

As Alexander Woolcott used to say, "lace" with 2 tablespoons of sherry. In other words, dribble the sherry over the crumbs. Have the oven temperature at 350 degrees and bake the fish 20 or 30 minutes.

The other method I sometimes use is to put 2 teaspoons of olive oil in a frying pan and go about the same procedure—salt, pepper, cream, crumbs and sherry. The frying is accomplished in 15 minutes. Do not turn the fish over. With moderate heat, the fish is cooked through and needs no particular watching. This will feed 4 people if they are not too hungry. Better get a pound and a half if appetites are husky.

Potato chips and a tossed green salad make this a real "quickie" for a hot day when you are too wilted to exert yourself more than necessary.

Kala Kukko

MY FINNISH friends on the other side of the cape have a way with fish that is different. It takes time, but the result is worthwhile and, as it is eaten cold, you can astound your friends with Kala Kukko on the buffet.

First, you make rye bread. 1 yeast cake is dissolved in 1 quart of lukewarm water. Add 1½ pounds of rye flour and stir until smooth. Let this rise overnight in a warm place.

Next morning stir in white flour, enough to make the dough

easy to handle. Add 1 teaspoon of salt. Now, let the dough rise again in a warm place. Punch down and knead the dough into a loaf. Let it rise again. Pat it flat on a floured board.

Lay filets of fish, preferably haddock, using 1½ pounds, on the dough. Sprinkle lightly with salt. Lay strips of salt pork on the fish. ½ pound of salt pork is plenty.

Fold over the edges of the dough to cover the filling and bake slowly at least an hour and a half in a moderate oven, 375 degrees.

When done, brush the top with butter.

This, served in slices, will feed as many as 8 or 10 if sliced thin. Most people hereabouts like a good fat slice, however.

Tuna Fish, Macaroni, and Cheese

THE ingredients for this delicious casserole may be kept on the emergency shelf and tossed together in short order.

First, cook a package of macaroni; you should have 4 cups of it when cooked.

Make a white sauce by melting 3 tablespoons of butter or margarine with 1 teaspoon of finely minced onion. Blend in 3 tablespoons of flour and gradually add 3 cups of milk. Stir and cook until thick and smooth. Add 2 tablespoons of catsup and ½ teaspoon of Worcestershire sauce.

Open 2 7-ounce cans of tuna fish or you can use 2 cups of it flaked. I pour boiling water over the tuna in a sieve to remove the oil.

Place half the macaroni, ½ cup of grated American cheese and 1 cup of fish in a buttered baking dish. Cover with half the white sauce. Repeat with the rest of the macaroni, fish, ½ cup of cheese and the rest of the white sauce. Top with 4 slices of bacon. Bake 30 minutes in a hot oven, 400 degrees. This serves 6 or 8.

You may substitute cooked noodles for the macaroni and 1 can of cream of mushroom soup thinned with 1 cup of milk for the white sauce. Buttered crumbs may take the place of the 4 strips of bacon. Either dish is very good, and may be assembled during the morning, between other duties.

Norwegian Fish Pudding

SCRAPE 1 pound of haddock filets from the skin with a knife, holding the skin firmly. It comes off more easily than you'd expect. Put the fish through the meat grinder 4 or 5 times. This makes 2 cups of ground fish. Put it in a good-sized bowl and mash with a wooden potato masher until it is doughy and pasty. The more it is mashed the better the pudding. The Norwegians turn out a fish pudding "soother than the creamy curd." The poet Keats can make you fairly dribble at the mouth.

To this mixture add 1 teaspoon of salt, ⅛ teaspoon of white pepper, 2 tablespoons of flour and a dash of nutmeg. Beat in 2 eggs, one at a time, using the electric beater or the regular egg beater. Beat well and then add ⅓ cup of melted butter, using part margarine if you must. I melt the butter in the baking dish, thus greasing it at the same time.

Then add 1 cup of top milk with a final good beating.

I use an earthen pudding dish or a fancy, tin, fish mold if the recipe is doubled. Sprinkle 1 teaspoon of fine dry bread crumbs over the bottom and sides. Pour in fish mixture gently. Sprinkle paprika on top. The dish can stand (covered) in the refrigerator until an hour and a half before dinner time. One hour before dinner, place the pudding dish in a shallow pan of hot water. Have the oven at 350 degrees and bake one hour. Serves 4.

This is firm enough to be turned out on a platter if you are using the fancy fish-shaped mold.

Serve with Dill sauce, made during an odd moment. Keep it in the double boiler ready to heat. It can stay on the back of the stove.

Heat ¾ cup of water in top of a double boiler over the flame. Put in 1 tablespoon of chopped chives. If you have to use onion instead, remove it from the liquid after 3 minutes of boiling. Add 3 tablespoons of lemon juice, ¼ teaspoon of salt, a dash of pepper.

In a bowl have 2 egg yolks slightly beaten. Gradually pour the hot liquid on them beating constantly. Add 2 tablespoons of butter or margarine, one at a time, while beating. Return to double boiler and add 2 tablespoons of chopped fresh dill and cook over boiling water until thick and smooth, never letting up on the beating. An egg-beater does the work effectively. Serves 4.

If no fresh dill is at hand, use dried dill and remove with the onion after it has boiled 3 minutes. Fresh dill grows easily in the garden and adds a cool zest to salads, boiled new potatoes and all fish dishes.

Salmon Soufflé

MELT 3 tablespoons of butter or margarine in a saucepan, blend in 3 tablespoons of flour. Gradually add 1 cup of milk and stir and cook until smooth and thick.

Add 1 cup of flaked canned salmon, free from juice, 1 teaspoon of salt and ½ teaspoon of paprika, 1 tablespoon minced parsley and the same of minced chives. You may use grated onion, 1 tablespoon, if you have no chives. Then add 2 teaspoons of lemon juice.

Beat 4 egg yolks and add to the mixture. If you are preparing this soufflé in the morning, store it in the refrigerator until 1½ hours before dinner. Beat the 4 egg whites until stiff but not dry. By the way, egg whites beat up better if they are not too cold. Room temperature is just right. Fold the egg whites into the first mixture just before baking. Heat the oven to 300 degrees and bake for 1½ hours. If you prefer the quick method, heat the oven to 425 degrees and bake the soufflé 25 minutes. This method produces a softer and creamier soufflé, but it must be eaten at once. It will serve 5 or 6.

Salmon Slice, Masked

DRAIN a can of salmon, remove bones and bits of fat. Place it on an ovenproof platter and saturate it with the juice of a lemon. Cover and heat for 10 minutes in a moderate oven, that is, 350 degrees.

Mask with a cream sauce made by melting 2 tablespoons of butter or margarine and blending in 3 tablespoons of flour. Gradually add 2 cups of rich milk and cook and stir until smooth and thick.

Have 2 hard-boiled eggs on hand. Chop the whites and add them to the cream sauce. Sieve the yolks and add half to the sauce. Sprinkle the other half on the salmon after you have masked it with the cream sauce.

This is a backhand way of explaining how I do this, but I have been thinking that this would be a good dinner after you went to the Symphony on Friday and your head was too full of echoing music to concentrate on cooking.

In this case, prepare the sauce before you leave the house. Have everything else ready and while the salmon is heating in the oven warm up the cream sauce, and a can of peas, or cook some frozen peas.

It is a lovely dinner to look at when the masked salmon is sprinkled with the sieved egg yolks and the green peas circle it. Have some potato chips and bring home some ice cream. Your dreamy condition won't be disturbed with rattling around the kitchen.

4 can be served.

Salmon and Rice Loaf

THIS loaf is served cold and fits into a supper menu or a summer lunch on the porch or terrace. Make it the day before.

Soften 1½ tablespoons of plain gelatin in ¼ cup of cold water. When it is dissolved pour over it ¾ cup of scalding hot milk, stir until completely dissolved.

Have 1 cup of cooked rice and mix it with 1 medium-sized can of salmon which you have freed from bones and skin and flaked. Season with 1 teaspoon of salt and ½ teaspoon paprika. Add 1 tablespoon melted butter or margarine. Now stir in the milk and gelatin, mix well and pour into a wet mold. A fancy fish-shaped mold makes a pretty dish. You turn it out on a platter and make wonderful fish eyes with thin slices of stuffed olives. Surround with billows of lettuce and parsley and lemon cut in any style your imagination suggests. Pass mayonnaise with it. Serves 4 or 5.

Finnan Haddie with Macaroni

IF YOU have leftover finnan haddie, all well and good. But if you are starting from scratch, bake the finnan haddie in milk almost to cover it until the fish readily separates into flakes. Bake slowly about 25 minutes. This recipe calls for 2 cups of the flaked fish.

Now you need 4 cups of cooked macaroni. 2 cups are laid on the bottom of a greased baking dish. Over this spread 1 cup of finnan haddie, ¼ cup of minced pimiento, ¼ cup of sliced olives, ½ teaspoon salt and a shake of pepper. Dot with butter or margarine generously. Repeat this process with the rest of the macaroni, fish, pimiento and olives and cover with cracker crumbs mixed with ½ cup of grated cheese. Over it all pour rich milk, enough to show through, but not to inundate the crumbs and cheese. Bake this in an oven 350 degrees for 1 hour or until it is brown and crusty on top.

This dish may be prepared and set aside until time to bake it. It makes a good meal for a cold winter night and feeds 6 easily. There may even be some leftover for the cat.

Spinach in the Benét manner goes well with this dinner. Cook a package of cleaned spinach in a very little water. Let it boil 10 minutes. Then set aside. 15 minutes before dinner, put the spinach in a colander over boiling water. The leaves will fluff up and the heat finishes the cooking.

Union Lane Scallops

This dish is a bachelor's specialty. Men are good cooks and they are adventurers in seasoning sauces.

Buy a pound of scallops. Rinse and drain them. Make a rich white sauce with 3 tablespoons of butter or margarine melted in a pan. Rub in 3 tablespoons of flour and gradually add 3 cups of rich milk. Part cream, of course, makes the sauce like velvet. Simmer and stir until thick and smooth. Add ½ teaspoon salt, ¼ teaspoon paprika, 1 drop of Tabasco sauce and ½ teaspoon Worcestershire sauce. Stir in some grated cheese, about ¼ cup, or more if you like. Cook until cheese has melted, which is only a minute or two.

If you plan to assemble this dish hours before serving time, keep the sauce cool and keep the scallops very cold. An hour before dinner heat the sauce in a double boiler. Rinse in cold water and drain the uncooked scallops and add them to the sauce. When they are hot enough, stir in 1 tablespoon of sherry. More, if your taste demands. Have the oven heated, in the meantime, to 350 degrees. Arrange the scallops and sauce in a greased baking dish. Sprinkle with bread crumbs, more grated cheese, and dot generously with butter or margarine. Bake for ¾ of an hour. This will serve 4.

This bachelor treats Finnan Haddie in the same way. Soak the fish overnight. In the morning drain it and cover with fresh water and simmer a few minutes until the fish flakes easily. Keep the pieces quite sizeable. Proceed as for Union Lane Scallops. 1 pound of finnan haddie with 3 cups of sauce is about right for 4 people.

Shrimp "Perlow" from Minorca

"PERLOW" is the way Southern cooks pronounce Pilau. This recipe calls for fresh shrimp, 2 pounds of them. To cook them, cover with boiling salted water and boil until they turn the delectable pink called "shrimp." Drain, cool in cold water and remove the shells with your fingers. Take out the black strip with a knife, and cut the shrimp in two. Medium-size shrimp give the best flavor. 2 cans of shrimp are equal to 2 pounds of the fresh. Clean the canned shrimp, if you use them instead of the fresh, in the same manner.

Fry 4 slices of bacon in a large pan until they are crisp. Break the slices into bits; a fork will do it nicely. Add 4 medium-sized onions, 1 small green or sweet red pepper, cut up, and if you live in the South, use 1 small datil pepper. Now, when these have cooked gently for 15 minutes, open a can of tomatoes and add enough water to equal 3½ cups. Find a heavy pot and transfer the mixture in the frying pan along with the shrimp to the heavy pot, then pour in the liquids and when it all comes to a boil, add 2 cups of washed rice. Cook very slowly until the rice is tender and each grain stands out distinct. If you desire, a pinch of thyme or other spices may be added. Salt to taste—the amount depends on you.

This Perlow cooks, after the rice is added, with no attention from the cook. The fire, of course, must be kept low under the pot. 4 or 5 will be served with this amount.

Shrimp in a Spaghetti Ring

COOK a package of thin spaghetti according to directions on the box. Drain. Butter a ring mold and make layers of spaghetti, ½ cup of finely chopped cheese, 1 tablespoon minced green pepper and the same amount of pimiento if you happen to have some on hand. The flecks of red and green look nice against the creamy color of the unmolded ring. Pour over the ring 1 cup of milk mixed with 3 beaten eggs and ½ teaspoon of salt. This can be baked now and heated later or it can wait until ¾ of an hour before dinner. Either way you choose, be sure to put the ring mold in a pan of hot water to bake ¾ of an hour. The oven should be 350 degrees.

The sauce for the shrimp is made in a saucepan. Cook in 2 or 3 tablespoons of butter or margarine, 1 teaspoon minced onion, 1 teaspoon minced green pepper. While cooking gently, toss in a leaf of basil and a sprig of tarragon. Remove later if they appear unsightly. In this mixture stir in 3 tablespoons of flour, 1 teaspoon salt and ⅛ teaspoon pepper. If you have fresh dill in the garden add 1 teaspoon of it chopped. Now that the flour is blended, gradually stir in 2 cups of rich milk. Cook over a gentle flame until thick and smooth. If you are preparing this sauce beforehand, pour it into the top of the double boiler. Later when you have heated it, add 1 jigger of sherry.

Clean a 7-ounce can of shrimp and store in the refrigerator. Add them to the hot sauce, just before serving and allow them to become hot but do not cook more than a few minutes or the shrimp will lose its faint tangy flavor.

When it is time to turn out the hot spaghetti ring, do it carefully on a large platter. Pour the shrimps in the center. Most likely the center will not be large enough for all the shrimps, so have the remainder in a bowl to serve with extra helpings. This recipe is enough for 4 or 5 people. It is awfully good, too.

Lobster Newburg

ACCORDING to some cooks this is not a true Newburg, but it is my best summer party dish. These proportions are for 4 people.

Make a thick white sauce. Melt 3 tablespoons of butter in a

saucepan, add ½ teaspoon of scraped onion and 2 leaves of fresh tarragon and a pinch of nutmeg. Stir in 3 tablespoons of flour and gradually add 2 cups of rich milk and 1 or 2 beaten eggs. Bring to a gentle boil, stirring continually, simmer a few minutes, season with salt and pepper.

Let the sauce cool. Then store it in the refrigerator until half an hour before dinner time. Heat it in the top of a large double boiler. When hot, add 1 pound of fresh lobster meat or use the tinned if you can't get fresh lobster. When it is all hot, pour in enough sherry to suit your taste, and stir well. Serve with boiled rice or toast.

The attention needed at the last moment is negligible and I always have my favorite dessert that needs no attention—Meringues with fruit and custard. This dessert is in another section.

Deviled Lobster

HAVE on hand 3 or 4 hard-boiled eggs and 2 cups of diced fresh lobster or the equivalent of canned lobster.

Melt 2 tablespoons of butter or margarine in a saucepan and blend in 2 tablespoons of flour. Gradually add 2½ cups of milk and cook until thick and smooth. Mash the yolks of the eggs or rub them through a sieve and mix thoroughly into the hot sauce. Cook a few minutes longer.

Cut the egg whites in slivers and toss them into the sauce along with 2 tablespoons of finely minced parsley, the same amount of chives or minced onion (not over a teaspoon of onion). Season with 1 teaspoon of salt, a sprinkle of paprika. Now add the lobster and 2 tablespoons of sherry.

Gently pour all this into a buttered casserole, a shallow one is best. Cover with ⅓ cup of bread crumbs and dot 2 tablespoons of butter or margarine over the top. Bake in a very hot oven, 500 degrees, for 10 minutes. If you wish, the baking may be delayed if the casserole is kept cool. Allow enough time for the oven to get hot and the casserole to warm to room temperature. Then bake it 10 minutes.

This is a good party dish and it will serve at least 8 people.

Lobster Stew

ALLOW ¼ of a pound of lobster meat to a person. You will serve this stew in bowls so measure bowls full of milk for each person. Heat the milk in the top of the double boiler, salt lightly, add a little paprika (1 teaspoon is plenty). Drop in a bit of bay leaf and don't forget to take it out before the lobster goes in. Add 1 teaspoon of catsup to each bowl of milk and the same of butter or margarine.

Put a lump of butter in a frying pan, as much as your budget allows, and dump in the lobster meat. Cook only to heat the meat through, and that is about 3 minutes. Add contents of this pan, melted butter and all, to the hot milk. Stir in 1 teaspoon of sherry to each bowl of milk. Serve at once.

If you wish, the milk can be enriched with a broth made from boiling the lobster bodies in water to cover. Enough water should be used so that after gentle boiling for half an hour you will be rewarded with a cup of the tangy broth.

It takes longer to tell about this than to do it. Melinna makes a specialty of this lobster stew and she is always in the living room with her guests while the stew is being made. Magic? Not at all, just careful planning and knowing exactly what she is about. Hot pilot crackers are served with the stew. A tossed salad, a simple dessert and coffee make it a memorable feast.

Codfish Chowder as Done in Connecticut

BUY 4 pounds of codfish and take along the tail, backbone and head. The fish is cut into small pieces and set aside and the head, tail and backbone are boiled in 2 cups of water for 5 minutes.

Dice 2 or 3 slices of salt pork and try out, adding towards the end, 2 sliced onions. Fry until a light brown. Strain the fat into a kettle and add 3 medium-sized potatoes peeled and cut wedge-shaped, or cubed if you are a real Connecticuter. Pour in 2 cups of hot water and cook for 5 minutes. Then add the liquid drained from the fishbones and the fish you already have cut into pieces about 1½ inches square. Let all this simmer under a cover for 15 minutes, season to taste with salt and pepper, add 3 tablespoons of butter or margarine and 2½ cups of strained canned tomatoes. Bring to bubbling heat.

If you are going to let this chowder stand on the back of the stove to ripen for a day, it will improve. Just before heating and serving stir in ½ cup of cracker crumbs.

This recipe will serve 4 or 5 amply, and it is a heartening meal for a cold winter day.

Gloucester Haddock Chowder

A HADDOCK weighing about 2 pounds should be cut into several pieces. Boil in salted water until the flesh will come off the bones easily. This takes only a few minutes. Drain, but save the water. Bone and skin the fish, keeping it in good-sized pieces.

Try out 3 or 4 slices of diced salt pork. Remove the crisp bits of pork, but keep them. In the hot fat, brown 1 large onion cut up. Then add 1½ cups of potatoes peeled and cut in wedges. Fastidious cooks demand the wedge-shaped potatoes because they say the point breaks off and thickens the chowder just enough. Cover the potatoes in the kettle with just enough water to cook them. As soon as the potatoes are tender, add the water the fish was cooked in, the pieces of fish and 1 quart of rich milk. Bring just to a boil. Salt and pepper to taste.

Old-timers used to soak common crackers (a type you find only in the East) in cold milk to soften them. The hot chowder was poured over them. Few do that nowdays. The chowder is served in bowls, with crisp pilot crackers in a separate dish. The pork bits are sprinkled over each serving of chowder. Everyone agrees that fish chowder improves with standing. Bring it to a good simmering heat before serving. This will serve 6.

Clam Chowder

1 PINT of clams out of the shell shortens the time of preparation. Separate the soft part from the necks. Put the necks through the food chopper.

Dice a slice of salt pork about 2 by 3 inches in size. Try out the tiny cubes in a good-sized kettle until crisp and pale brown. Remove the scraps and set aside. Mince a small onion into the fat and cook until soft, but not brown.

Peel and dice 3 medium-sized potatoes and add to the onions with enough water to cover. Simmer until tender with half a bay leaf and ½ teaspoon of salt. The chopped necks are added with a quart of milk and the whole allowed to come to a boil before the soft parts of the clams are put in. Cook one minute longer. Remove from fire, cover and let stand all day if you like. All chowder experts agree that standing develops the flavors. Just before dinner bring to a boil, taste to see if it needs more salt. Pour into a tureen, sprinkle the pork scraps on the top and serve at once with pilot crackers. New Englanders, now and then, like sour pickles with their chowder. Serves 6.

This is a hearty, filling meal and salad can be skipped if you like, with a leisurely progress from the chowder to a handsome, juicy apple pie still warm from a gentle heating in the oven and smelling divinely of nutmeg and cinnamon. Flanked with wedges of assorted cheese and cups of strong coffee, you can discuss the feud that rages up and down the New England coast as to whether chowder should be desecrated with the addition of tomatoes, or not.

Vegetable Chowder

You start out as you do for fish or clam chowder by dicing 2 or 3 slices of salt pork. Try them out in a deep kettle. When the bits of pork are crisp, remove from the kettle and save them. Into the hot fat dump 1 cup of diced carrots, 1 cup of diced celery, 1 cup diced potatoes and, if you like turnip, 1 cup of turnip diced. You may use other vegetables. I like lima beans instead of turnip. Add 1 cup of beef or chicken stock which may be made with bouillon cubes. Cook until the vegetables are tender. Keep the cover on the kettle while this is going on. Now pour in a can of tomato soup and ⅛ teaspoon of soda.

As soon as this is hot, add 4 cups of milk. If you prefer a thicker chowder, mix 2 tablespoons of flour with a little cold water and stir into the chowder and allow to boil until thick. Herb addicts may drop in a leaf of basil or any other favorite seasoning when the vegetables are cooking. Taste the chowder to see if it needs salt. Now, allow the kettle to cool and the flavors to ripen overnight if you like. But keep it cool. Bring to bubbling heat and serve with pilot crackers that have been lightly spread with butter or margarine and warmed to a crispness in the oven.

This chowder is a stand-by along the Eastern seaboard. It will serve 6. Sprinkle the tureen with the bits of salt pork that you rescued from the kettle.

Stuffed Peppers and Tomatoes with Sauce

Scoop out the pulp from 4 large tomatoes. Cut two large sweet green peppers in half and clean out the seeds.

Mix the tomato pulp with 1 pound of chopped lamb, or beef mixed with lamb. Add ½ cup of raw rice, 1 teaspoon salt, ¼ teaspoon pepper and ¼ cup of minced parsley. Stuff tomatoes and peppers with this mixture. If any is leftover, tuck it between the peppers and tomatoes. Put in a flat pan or casserole, add hot water to reach about an inch above the bottom of the dish. Cook on top of the stove until the rice is cooked.

This is the way it is done in George Demetrious' kitchen where a large husky coal range is always going. You may bake this dish in a moderate oven until the rice is done, which will take about an hour. The peppers and tomatoes may already be in the dish hours ahead of time, waiting only to be popped in the oven unless you, too, have a stove going in the kitchen.

The Egg and Lemon Sauce raises this dish to epicurean heights.

Beat 3 eggs and add the juice of ½ lemon. Take juice from the casserole in a large ladle, in your left hand. With the right hand stir egg and lemon with a spoon and add the hot juice drop by drop slowly. The ladle holds probably ¾ of a cup of liquid.

Pour this sauce over the casserole. Cook about 5 minutes or until the eggs are cooked. This sounds more difficult than it is. Any cook knows how to use both hands at once, so don't hesitate to concoct this delicious sauce. I run out of adjectives when I attempt to describe the meal done in this Greek style.

Serve one tomato and ½ a pepper to each. The Demetrious family is 4.

Vegetable Loaf

WHEN the vegetable garden is producing more than you can put up or give away, serve the vegetables in a loaf. I used for this loaf, ½ cup of finely chopped celery, 2 cups of cut-up tomatoes; ½ an onion, 1 carrot and 1 green pepper were put through the grinder. A tiny bouquet of fresh herbs, basil, tarragon or whatever you fancy, gives the loaf piquancy. Add 2 tablespoons of peanut butter or use ½ cup of peanuts ground with the carrot and pepper. Now add ½ cup of dry bread crumbs. Mix and moisten with ¼ cup of milk and 1 beaten egg. Season with 1 teaspoon of salt and ⅛ teaspoon of pepper. Bake 1 hour in an oven 350 degrees. This will serve 4.

Other vegetables, such as corn cut from the cob and lima beans that have been cooked, may be added to the mixture. The mixture should have a mush-like consistency before baking. The loaf needs a sauce to pep it up. A can of undiluted tomato soup or a dehydrated spaghetti sauce prepared according to directions on the package, is suitable.

The loaf can be mixed in the morning and left, covered with wax paper, until time to bake it. Of course I like cheese with nearly everything, and the loaf can be topped generously with grated cheese before baking. This will serve 4.

Spaghetti with Eggplant Sauce

THIS is an interesting meatless sauce. You start out with a quart of peeled and diced eggplant. A medium-sized eggplant is about right. Soak the cubes in water 10 minutes.

Put 2 tablespoons of bacon fat in a heavy saucepan, add 1 clove of garlic minced, 1 green pepper chopped and 2 fresh basil leaves. Cook until tender. Add 1 can of tomatoes, 1 teaspoon of salt and

¼ teaspoon of pepper. This should simmer slowly. If the pan is covered and the heat is gentle, the sauce needs no stirring and other duties about the house can be tended to.

If you are going to have very little time before dinner, cook a package of spaghetti according to directions on the box. Drain and rinse with cold water. Leave it in the colander. A non-rusting colander must be used. Aluminum is best. Cover with a clean towel.

A few minutes before dinner time, heat the sauce. Lower the colander of spaghetti into a kettle of boiling water, or else pour plenty of boiling water over it. The spaghetti will be hot and ready to eat. Serves 4.

I learned this trick from a woman who lived many years in France. It seems a radical departure from our usual method, but it works.

Of course you can put the cooked spaghetti in a casserole, cover it with the sauce and bake it an hour in an oven 350 degrees. Either way it is good, and should have grated Parmesan cheese sprinkled over it when it is served.

Scalloped Eggplant

THIS is a whole meal and demands only some crunchy bread to round it out.

Peel a medium-sized eggplant and cut it into 1-inch cubes. Cover with cold salted water and cook until it is just tender. Drain and mix with 1 cup of very finely chopped celery, one small onion, likewise chopped fine. If you have basil growing in a pot, add 1 leaf, minced, or a whiff of dried basil. Drain a can of tomatoes and add to the mixture along with a green pepper sliced in thin rings and 1 cup of diced raw ham. Add 1 teaspoon salt and ⅛ teaspoon of pepper. Then, stir in either a cup of Wheaties or bread crumbs. Ladle this into a baking dish, dot with margarine or butter and sprinkle liberally with grated cheese. Bake at 350 degrees for 1¼ hours. This makes a hearty meal for 4 people. The dish can be assembled hours before baking.

Broccoli Soufflé

For a meatless meal this soufflé is perfect and very pretty to look at. It uses 1 cup of leftover broccoli.

Melt 3 tablespoons of butter or margarine in a saucepan and blend in 3 tablespoons of flour. Gradually stir in 1 cup of milk and stir and cook until smooth and thick. Add 1 teaspoon of salt, a few grains of nutmeg and 1 teaspoon of lemon juice. Chop the cooked broccoli, and measure 1 cup.

Beat the yolks of 4 eggs, add the first mixture and allow to cool. If you are assembling the soufflé hours before time to serve it, keep it in a cool place. 1½ hours before serving time, beat the 4 egg whites until stiff but not dry. There is a fine distinction here. Fold the egg whites gently into the first mixture and bake in a slow oven, 300 degrees, for 1½ hours. The quick method calls for an oven heated to 425 degrees and 25 minutes of baking.

Some people think broccoli always calls for Hollandaise sauce. It is very good with this soufflé and so is a cheese sauce. 5 or 6 people can be served with this recipe.

Rice with Pineapple

Cook 2 cups of rice according to directions on the package. Drain and arrange in layers in a buttered casserole. Between each layer sprinkle brown sugar, using ¾ of a cup in all. A tiny sprinkle of salt is advised. Cut 6 slices of canned pineapple into bits and scatter between the layers. Top with a circle of pineapple and a few wedges, making a nice design. Pour 1 cup of pineapple juice on the rice. Bake 20 minutes in a moderate oven. This can be prepared in the morning.

This rice casserole is always served at the Cady's buffet suppers. One of Harrison's best stories is about a little boy who followed the adventures of Peter Rabbit. Harrison draws the pictures for the funny page of the New York *Herald Tribune*. The youngster came to Rockport and begged to be taken to see Harrison Cady. When he saw him at the door of his studio he exclaimed in deep dismay, "Why! It's only a man!" He had expected to see a live rabbit, appearing just as appealing as Harrison draws him. But the least acquaintance with Harrison Cady is richly rewarding, even though he isn't a rabbit!

To go back to the rice and pineapple. This recipe will serve 6, and goes well with cold ham or roast pork.

Mexican Macaroni

Cook a package of macaroni until tender, according to directions on the box. Drain. Make a sauce of 3 tablespoons of butter melted in a saucepan. Add 3 tablespoons of flour and blend well. Add 2 cups of milk gradually and cook and stir until thick and smooth. Add ¼ teaspoon of salt and ¼ to ½ a pound of cheese, the amount depending on the ripe, old age of the cheese and your liking for lots of cheese. Stir until melted. Add the macaroni to this sauce along with ¾ cup of raisins and ¼ cup of minced pimiento. Place in a baking dish. Cover with ½ cup of cracker crumbs tossed in a pan with 2 tablespoons of butter until well coated. Bake at your convenience for ½ an hour in a moderate oven. This serves 4, and doubled it is a favorite dish for buffet suppers. The raisins and pimiento make macaroni devotees smack their lips with surprised appreciation.

Mushrooms à la King

IF YOU are asking a few people to stop in after the movie, give them mushrooms à la king. It can be ready in the double boiler and all you do is to heat it and have someone make toast—good and crisp toast, if you please.

Chop 3 stalks of tender celery finely and cook them in a little water until tender. Drain. Slice 3 hard-boiled eggs very thin.

Brush the tops of a pound of mushrooms. Cut into slices and sauté in 3 tablespoons of butter or margarine for 10 minutes, or until brown. Stir in 2 tablespoons of flour and when smooth, gradually add 2 cups of rich milk and season with salt, pepper and paprika. Cook slowly and stir until the mixture is thick. Add the celery and eggs and, if you have them, ¼ cup of sliced ripe olives.

This will serve only 4. When you reheat, do not allow it to boil. Flavor with 2 tablespoons of sherry.

Spanish Rice

TO DO this as I saw it done, use a large earthenware casserole. You must have a very low flame, of course. Gently warm the casserole and pour in ¼ cup of olive oil. When this is hot put in 1 large onion and 1 green pepper chopped finely and 1 teaspoon salt. Stir gently now and then for a few minutes. Wash and dry 1 cup of rice. Stir it into the casserole and brown. Keep on stirring until it is brown.

Now add slowly 2 cups of hot water and bits of any leftover meat. Ham is good. Stir until well mixed. Cover closely and cook over a low flame without stirring for about an hour.

This was done by an experienced cook, one of those who says to use a little of this and a little of that. No one ever quite reaches the perfect result, but these directions produce a mighty fine meal for 3 or 4 people.

Spaghetti with Burgundy

THE use of wine in cookery has long been known in Europe and we are just beginning to discover what it can do to a plebeian dish.

First have 3 cups of cooked spaghetti. Cut in little bits enough American cheese to make ¾ of a cup.

In 3 tablespoons of fat (bacon is best) fry 1 minced onion, 1 minced clove of garlic and 1 minced green pepper. When they are soft and lightly browned add ½ pound of chopped beef. Stir and cook until meat is seared. Add 2½ cups of chopped fresh tomatoes or the same amount of solid, canned tomatoes. Season with 1 teaspoon salt, ¼ teaspoon pepper and 1 teaspoon sugar. It is a good idea to use a little sugar in dishes calling for tomatoes. Simmer this mixture 30 minutes over a low flame. Pour in ½ cup of Burgundy wine. Mix with the spaghetti and cheese and pour into a greased casserole.

This should bake 1 hour in an oven heated to 325 degrees. You may set it aside and bake hours later. If you keep it overnight store it in the refrigerator.

This is a hearty dinner for 4 or 5 people.

Mexican Bean Pot

DO SOMETHING about Saturday night baked beans. Try this once and you will do it again.

You may start with dried kidney beans, soaked overnight and boiled until just tender, but it is much easier to open 2 cans of kidney beans and put them in a bean pot or casserole with the following ingredients.

Mix together 2 tablespoons of bacon fat, a clove of garlic minced, 1 pinch English thyme, and 1 of rosemary. These last-named herbs are optional. 1 small bay leaf, 2 cloves, 1 teaspoon salt, 1 teaspoon dry mustard, a pinch of cayenne pepper, 2 table-spoons of vinegar or, what is better if you have it, ½ cup of juice from pickled pears, peaches or watermelon pickles. Slice 1 onion extremely thin.

Mingle this savory mixture with the beans and put it in the bean pot or casserole. Bake it for an hour in a slow oven, 275 de-grees. Then place 3 or 4 slices of bacon on top and pour over it ¼ cup of good strong coffee and allow it to bake until the bacon is crisp. Have the oven 400 degrees. If you are not serving the beans at once, let the dish stand until half an hour before dinner. Then bring it to a good piping heat in a hot oven which will take 15 or 20 minutes. Now add 1 jigger of brandy or sherry or red wine and let the bean pot stay in the hot oven a few minutes longer while the brandy or sherry permeates the savory depths of the bean pot. Serve at once. This should serve 4 to 6.

Curry Squash

WHEN the garden is flourishing, this vegetable dish is easy to pre-pare and serve with sliced cold meats on a hot evening when too much cooking is to be avoided.

You can fix this in the morning and have it ready to pop into the oven later.

Cut into small pieces 3 good-sized summer squash. Boil in a little salted water until soft. Drain well and mash. Add 1 teaspoon (or more to taste) of curry powder, ½ cup of milk and 1 beaten egg. Mix thoroughly and pour into a greased casserole. When you have the oven heated to 350 degrees, bake the squash for about ½ an hour.

The flavor of curry enhances what Sara Henderson Hay says is a pallid dish. She is a poet, and invented this dish, so she may call it pallid if she likes. It will serve 4.

Crumbed Eggs

I WAS doubtful about this recipe until I tried it and found it awfully good. The novelty of this dish will appeal to anyone who gets tired of eggs in the usual ways of serving them.

Cut in half 6 hard-boiled eggs, lengthwise. Remove the yolks and mash them well. Mix in ¼ teaspoon of dry mustard, 3½ teaspoons mayonnaise and 1 hard-boiled egg chopped as fine as possible. Fill the egg whites with the mixture. Roll them gently in 1 cup of fine bread crumbs, then 1 well-beaten egg to which 1 teaspoon of water has been added. Roll again in crumbs. Place on greased baking sheet, dot with butter or margarine and bake 20 minutes in an oven heated to 350 degrees. A tomato sauce goes well with the eggs, or a white sauce made perky with finely chopped chives and parsley. This dish can be ready to pop in the oven at any time.

I have sautéed the eggs in margarine in a frying pan and found the result satisfactory. One egg each is enough, so 6 eggs will serve 6 people unless they have whopping big appetites.

Turkish Omelet

THIS omelet will astonish you, but try it and find out how delightful it really is.

Separate 5 eggs. Beat the whites until stiff. Beat the yolks until thick and creamy. I use an electric beater and beat the whites first. I do not wash the beater but use it with flecks of white sticking to it for the yolks. To the yolks, when beaten, add ¼ cup of boiling water and ½ teaspoon of salt. Combine gently with the whites using a folding-over motion with a large spoon.

In a good-sized frying pan melt 1 tablespoon of butter or margarine and pour in the egg mixture. Keep the heat low, and when a spatula craftily inserted under the omelet shows that the bottom has browned, place it under the broiler until the top sets and is ever so faintly browned. Fold the omelet gently and persuade it to slip onto a hot platter.

In the meantime, have ½ a cup of honey heating over hot water. Pour the honey over the omelet and sprinkle with ½ cup of toasted cashew nuts.

This omelet, of course, cannot be prepared ahead of time but it is done in a jiffy and is a very satisfying meal for 4 people.

Scalloped Eggs

HARD-BOILED eggs are usually classed with picnic fare. But the ordinary stuffed egg halves, pinned together with a toothpick and wrapped in wax paper, become something out of this world when scalloped.

The recipe can be increased vastly and lends itself well to a buffet party when you want one hot dish that takes little time to prepare.

4 people will need 4 hard-boiled eggs. Cut in half after the shell is removed, mash the yolks and mix with 6 teaspoons of deviled ham and a pinch of salt if you think it is needed. Some brands of deviled ham are saltier than others, so taste before adding more salt.

Make a white sauce. Melt 2 tablespoons of butter or margarine and mix in 4 tablespoons of flour. Blend gradually with 2½ cups of rich milk. Cook and stir until smooth and thick. Add some zippy cheese, as much as you like, from ½ cup to 1 cup or a little more. It depends on the strength of the cheese and your personal liking for strong cheese. Stir until the cheese is melted. Chopped chives and parsley add color and flavor.

Arrange egg halves in a greased baking dish, pour the sauce over them and sprinkle lightly with buttered cracker crumbs or a prepared corn muffin mix. Bake 20 minutes in an oven heated to 400 degrees.

This dish can be prepared far in advance and kept cool until time to bake it. The top should be bubbly and brown, not a dark brown, but toasty brown.

Egg Casserole

THIS is one of the best-tasting egg dishes I have come upon. The casserole can be prepared any time and set aside to bake later in the day.

Mince 2 tablespoons each of onions and green peppers. Fry them gently in 2 tablespoons of fat until tender but not brown.

In a saucepan, melt 2 tablespoons of butter or margarine. Add 2 tablespoons of flour. Rub smooth and gradually add 1 cup of milk. Stir and cook over low heat until thick and smooth. Add ½ teaspoon of salt and a few grains of pepper.

Drain a No. 2 can of tomatoes and add the thick part to the sauce. Stir in ¼ teaspoon of chili powder.

Slice 4 or 5 hard-boiled eggs and gently stir them into the sauce. Pour in a buttered casserole or baking dish. Cover with ½ cup of buttered bread crumbs mixed with ½ cup of grated cheese.

When you bake this, have the oven medium hot, 350 degrees, and bake until thoroughly heated through. 20 minutes should do the trick. This will serve 4.

Easter Supper of Curried Eggs

EGGS are always plentiful at this time of year and this is a fascinating way to serve them. It is a complete meal in itself and it is very little work. The recipe can be increased to serve many more.

First, have 6 hard-boiled eggs, if you plan to serve 4 people.

Curry sauces vary and when you find a good one, stick to it.

In a large saucepan cook 2 minced onions in 2 tablespoons of margarine or butter until soft but not brown. Stir in 2 tablespoons of flour and blend until smooth. Gradually add 2 cups of liquid. Use 1 cup of chicken stock and 1 cup of rich milk. Bouillon cubes will make the stock. Or, you may use all milk. Cook over low heat until thick and smooth. Add ½ cup of seedless raisins and ½ cup of drained crushed pineapple. You may substitute a peeled chopped apple for the pineapple. Add the juice of ¼ lemon and a strip of lemon peel. Stir constantly. Add a little salt, not over ¼ teaspoon.

Mix 2 tablespoons of curry powder with a little water to make a paste. Mix this into the sauce. Simmer over a low flame for 15 or 20 minutes. Taste to see if it needs more salt.

Heat this sauce later in a double boiler. Allow 20 minutes for it to get hot. Add the sliced hard-boiled eggs. Serve with dry, fluffy rice and an assortment of condiments. Here is where the fun comes in. You take small helpings of the condiments and pile them on top of the curried eggs and rice and if you like, mix them all together or eat your way around the plate having a different adventure with each combination of flavors.

In little dishes have grated coconut, chopped salted peanuts, chopped green pepper, watermelon pickles, fried onions, the kind that come in cans, diced candied ginger, dried figs, and chutney. In some cities you can buy all the condiments used in India.

Alabama Casserole

THIS is a grand Sunday supper dish. It can be assembled during the day and left ready to pop into the oven. Have on hand 6 hard-boiled eggs.

Mix in a large bowl 1 can of tomato soup, 1 can of drained green peas, 1 small can of pimiento cut up, 1 small can of sliced mushrooms, 1 cup of finely diced celery, 1 green pepper diced, and 1 cup of grated cheese.

Now, make a cream sauce. Melt 3 tablespoons of butter or margarine and blend in 3 tablespoons of flour. Gradually add 1½ cups of rich milk. Stir and cook until thick and smooth. Season with 1 tablespoon of Worcestershire sauce.

Select a handsome casserole and put a layer of the first mixture in the casserole, then a layer of cream sauce, a layer of sliced eggs and continue. Have eggs on the top layer. Sprinkle liberally with buttered crumbs and bake 30 minutes in a moderate oven, 350 degrees.

This will serve 6 people generously.

Cheese Soufflé

THIS cheese soufflé can be started in the morning. Melt 3 tablespoons of butter or margarine, add 3 tablespoons of flour and blend well. Gradually add 1 cup of milk and cook, while stirring constantly until thick and smooth. Add 1 scant teaspoon of salt and a few grains of cayenne.

Add 1⅔ cups of grated American cheese and stir over a low fire until the cheese is melted. Remove from the fire. Beat 4 egg yolks and add to the first mixture and set aside to cool.

An hour and a half before dinner, beat the egg whites stiff but not dry and fold the cheese mixture into the whites. If the cheese mixture seems a bit too thick to fold in easily, beat it first and then fold it into the egg whites. The idea is not to use too much action in blending the two.

Pour gently into a greased 1½-quart casserole and bake in an oven heated to 300 degrees for an hour and a half. This slow-baked soufflé will hold up 15 minutes longer if the family is delayed.

If you wish to serve the soufflé in a shorter time it can be baked in a hot oven, 425 degrees for 25 minutes. But serve it at once or it will flop.

Cheese Sandwich Soufflé

THIS is a foolproof soufflé, easy to prepare. It needs no last-minute attention and it is very good, especially for a hearty lunch or supper dish.

Cut the crusts from 8 slices of bread. Place 4 slices in the bottom of a buttered baking dish. Over the bread, slice ¼ pound of American cheese, sometimes called rat-trap cheese. Cover with 4 slices of bread. Beat 3 eggs slightly and add 2 cups of milk, ½ teaspoon of salt, a shake of pepper and paprika. If you use a very tiny pinch of powdered sage you have something tantalizing in the taste. Pour this liquid over the cheese and bread. Put it in the refrigerator to chill for at least an hour. All morning is not too long.

Bake in an oven heated to 350 degrees for 35 minutes. By this time it should be puffed up like a proper soufflé. The dish will serve 4 people.

Julekage

DISSOLVE 2 cakes of yeast in ½ cup of lukewarm water. Pour 3 cups of scalding hot milk over ½ cup of butter or margarine. When it is lukewarm, add the yeast and ¾ cup of sugar. Add 2 teaspoons of salt and enough flour to make a batter. Beat well for 10 minutes. The amount of flour is difficult to state, but the dough should be like a thick pancake batter. Add 2 well-beaten eggs, one at a time, beating thoroughly after each addition. Add ½ cup of currants, ½ cup of chopped citron, ¾ cup of chopped raisins, ½ cup of candied cherries cut up and ½ teaspoon of powdered cardamom seeds.

Add flour, enough to make a dough easily handled. Knead on a floured board until it does not stick to the fingers. Place in a greased bowl, covered, and set to rise in a warm place, away from drafts. When the dough has risen to double in bulk, knead it down again. Let it rise again until light and then shape it into loaves and place in greased pans. Brush the top of loaves with egg white.

When the loaves have doubled in bulk, bake them in a moderate oven, 350 degrees, for 35 or 40 minutes. After removing from the oven, brush crusts with melted butter or margarine and sprinkle with sugar and cinnamon.

This makes wonderful toast for holiday breakfasts. You will probably decide to make this bread often, not waiting for Christmas to roll around again.

Portuguese Easter Bread

THE first time I made this wonderful bread I used a very large recipe and I had so much bread that I ran around the neighborhood Easter morning distributing it. The Portuguese do the same when they have the ancient Crowning ceremony in Gloucester in June. The bread is then made in large wreaths that slip over the arm, and an armful of bread is carried around to the poor of the community. I have seen these wreaths tied with red satin ribbon. They are auctioned after the feast.

Dissolve 1 yeast cake in ½ cup of lukewarm water. Scald 1 pint of milk and pour it over 2 tablespoons of lard and ¼ pound of butter or margarine to melt it. Beat 6 eggs, add 1 cup of sugar, 1½ teaspoons salt. When the milk is lukewarm add the yeast and egg mixture.

Mix as you would for any bread, with enough flour to make a stiff dough. Knead on a floured board until it does not stick to the fingers. Place in a greased bowl and cover with a towel.

Set in a warm place to rise. You may let it rise overnight. In the morning, early, cut it down and let rise again.

You may not wish to let this rise overnight. In that case, the rising may be hastened by placing the bowl of dough over warm water.

After the second rising, take some of the dough and shape it in a round loaf, pat until it is 2 inches thick. Wash 5 eggs and make depressions in the dough, place an egg in the center depression, and the other 4 eggs in place, as north, east, south and west.

Take a strip of dough and roll it in the palms and stretch it. Place one end of this strip over the north egg. Moisten the end, press it into the dough and bring the strip down over the center egg and over the south egg. Moisten and press the end into the dough. Do the same from east to west. Place loosely over the eggs.

With a shears, pink all around the rim of loaf and also on the strips. Cover and let rise. Bake in a hot oven, 400 degrees, until done. This is a very delicate bread and it will bake quickly. Watch it. It may be done in 25 to 30 minutes.

The cross and the eggs are only used for Easter. The eggs will be hard-cooked.

The rest of the dough may be shaped into loaves if you do not wish to make more than one round Easter loaf.

Nisu, Finnish Coffee Bread

HEAT 1 pint of milk, and when it is lukewarm dissolve ½ yeast cake in it. Then add 2 beaten eggs and 1 cup of sugar, ½ teaspoon salt and 8 cardamom seeds, crushed. A word of explanation in regard to the cardamom seeds might not be amiss. The seeds are encased in a thin pod. Break the pod, take out the tiny, dark seeds. Crush them in a stout cloth, using a hammer.

White flour is now sifted into the liquid. The amount is not to be exactly determined. Keep on adding flour until the dough can be easily handled. Knead until the dough stops sticking to the fingers. Mrs. Natti says this is very important. Put the dough in a large bowl.

Let the dough rise in a warm place, covered with a towel. It ought to double in bulk. Punch down, cut into three pieces and roll them into strips. Braid together, lay in a pan. Let it rise again and then bake in a moderate oven, 350 degrees, 30 to 40 minutes. After baking, brush it with liquid made of coffee and sugar and sprinkle with sugar.

Hungarian Coffee Cake

This is a baking-day treat from a cosy little parsonage over in Annisquam. It is very easy to make and it has an appearance unlike any coffee cake I ever saw before.

Scald 1 cup of milk. Add 1 tablespoon shortening and when it has cooled to lukewarm, add 1 tablespoon sugar, 1 teaspoon salt and 1 cake of yeast that has been dissolved in ¼ cup of warm water. Stir to mix and add enough sifted bread flour to make a medium stiff dough. I find that 3 heaping cups is about right. I do this in the large kettle in which I scalded the milk. Cover, and set in a warm place to raise double its bulk. Then cut it down and knead on a floured board. Cut off bits as large as a walnut and form them into balls in your hands. Dip in a mixture of cinnamon and sugar and then in melted shortening. Crisco, Spry or margarine are suitable. Grease a round tube pan, about 8 or 9 inches across, and pile the balls on top of one another. Let rise in a warm place until almost double in bulk. Bake 45 minutes in an oven heated to 375 degrees. You may add raisins and nuts to the dough, if you wish. When done, turn out of pan, and to serve, separate the balls with a fork.

Next time I make this coffee cake I am going to sprinkle plenty of brown sugar between the balls. This will make the sticky, sweet caramel that tastes so good.

Meringues with Fruit and Custard

MERINGUES are made the day before and kept in a tin box. They will keep almost a week. Whip 3 egg whites stiff and gradually beat in 1 cup of sifted, granulated sugar. Add 1 teaspoon vanilla and ½ teaspoon vinegar. Form into 6 meringues on waxed paper on the back of a cooky tin. Bake at 250 degrees for 1 hour.

Make a custard of the 3 egg yolks beaten slightly. Add 2 cups of milk and ¼ cup of sugar. Cook in a double boiler until it coats the spoon. I thicken it a little with 1 teaspoon cornstarch moistened with a little cold milk. Stir this in the hot custard and stir until it is thick. Cool. Flavor with 1 teaspoon vanilla or ¼ teaspoon almond and ¼ teaspoon of vanilla. The combination suggests pistachio. Keep in the refrigerator. Canned peaches, black cherries, pineapple, apricots or fresh fruit are arranged in dessert dishes before serving. The meringue is in the center, or on top of the fruit. Pour the chilled custard around it.

Honey and Sherry on Fruit

FRUIT for dessert is refreshing, winter or summer. Try fruit with honey and sherry. Heat ½ cup of honey over hot water until it is very thin. Pour in ¼ cup of sherry or a dry white wine and stir until it has blended. Pour over prepared fruit. Berries, bananas, fresh pineapple or peaches are suitable, separately or mixed. Chill well before serving.

Spiced Apple Snow

SPRINKLE 1 tablespoon of plain gelatin over ¼ cup of cold water. After 5 minutes add 1 cup of boiling water and stir until dissolved. Chill in the refrigerator.

Peel a large apple and grate it on a fine grater. Add a tiny pinch of cinnamon and the same of nutmeg, 3 tablespoons of lemon juice or a mixture of lime and lemon juice. Add ¼ cup of sugar. When the gelatin is cold, add it to this mixture and chill again until stiff. When it has reached that stage, beat 3 egg whites with a few grains of salt until they stand in peaks. Fold in ¼ cup of sugar, and beat a minute longer. Whip the stiffened gelatin with an egg beater until foamy. Fold in the egg whites, pour into a mold that has been rinsed in cold water.

Chill until very firm. Turn out on a dessert plate and serve with a custard made from the 3 egg yolks, 1½ cups of milk and 3 tablespoons of sugar cooked in a double boiler until it coats the back of a spoon. When cool, flavor with brandy or rum or a mixture of vanilla and almond.

This will serve 6.

Fruit Salad with West Indian Dressing

IN A saucepan, mix 4 tablespoons of water, 3 tablespoons of sugar and 2 tablespoons of butter. Let it come to a boil and get just the least bit stringy when you test it with a spoon, as you do jelly. Take it from the fire and when it has cooled a little, but is not cold, stir in rapidly 1 tablespoon of lemon juice. Pour it over fruit which has been prepared and mixed together in a bowl. Set the dish in the refrigerator. Serve when quite cold. The dressing will be found to have spread a delicate glaze over the fruit.

Do not use fruit that is too juicy or it will ruin the glaze which should be found on the fruit after a thorough chilling. Oranges should be drained before adding if they are inclined to be drippy.

Bananas, dates, drained canned pineapple, apples, even the much-ridiculed marshmallows are a joy to discover in this salad bowl.

This is enough dressing to cover a salad for 4 or 5 people.

Lemon Pie

HAVE a baked crust ready. I attempt no directions for pie crust, it is a touchy business and I am not an expert.

Beat 5 egg yolks until thick and pale. Gradually sift in ¾ cup of sugar and continue beating. Add the juice of 2 large lemons, or the juice of 2½ smaller lemons. Cook in a double boiler until mixture holds its shape, stirring continually. This takes about 15 minutes. Place over cold water to cool.

Beat 3 egg whites until stiff and fold the cooled custard into the egg whites. Turn into a baked pie shell. Top with a meringue made of 2 egg whites beaten until stiff, then add 2 tablespoons of sugar. Pile on top of custard and place in a hot oven 500 degrees, 3 to 5 minutes or until lightly browned. This lemony, golden mist topped with ambrosial clouds puts all other lemon pies to shame.

Graham Icebox Pudding

LINE a bread pan or an oblong pan with wax paper from the inside of a cracker box. Fit graham crackers on the bottom. Pour a layer of chocolate pudding over them. Cover with a layer of crackers. Repeat and finish with crackers on top. Two layers of pudding is about right for my pan. Cover with waxed paper and chill all day or overnight in the refrigerator. Serve in squares with whipped cream or a thick, boiled custard made with a package of vanilla pudding, using 3 cups of milk instead of the usual 2 cups.

Chocolate Filling for Pudding

4 SQUARES of chocolate cut in pieces and 1¼ cups of milk are heated in a double boiler. When the chocolate is melted, beat with rotary egg beater until smooth. Sift ¼ cup of flour with 1 cup of sugar; add a small amount of the chocolate mixture and stir until smooth. Return to double boiler and cook until thick and smooth, stirring continually. Add 2 tablespoons of butter and 1½ teaspoons of vanilla. Use while slightly warm because then it sticks to the graham crackers better.

Rice Pudding with Oranges

YEARS ago I clipped this recipe from the New York *Sun*. It is a variation of rice pudding that gives it an honorable place on a party menu.

First, boil ½ cup of rice in lots of water, as you always do. Drain it and put through a ricer. That is what makes this dessert unusual. Stir in ½ cup of sugar, the juice and grated rind of 2 small oranges.

Have soaking ⅓ box of plain gelatin or 1 tablespoon, to be accurate, in ⅔ cup of cold water. When soft, dissolve it over hot water and then mix it with the rice. Let it cool. Then fold in 1 pint of cream whipped stiff. Turn into a wet mold and chill.

Serve with shredded orange pulp and juice. This makes enough dessert for 6 people.

Brown Betty

THIS particular Brown Betty is served by one of New York's busy young editors who often entertains authors in her own apartment. It always brings forth loud cheers.

This is how she does it. Cut off the edges of 5 slices of whole-wheat bread; then cut them in small squares and fry in about 3 tablespoons of butter or margarine, turning them in order to soak up all the butter or margarine.

Peel and cut in small pieces enough apples to fill 3 cups.

Mix ½ teaspoon cinnamon, ½ teaspoon nutmeg and ½ cup of sugar.

Place alternate layers of bread squares and apples in a baking dish, pouring a bit of the spiced sugar over each layer. Sprinkle a little lemon juice as you go along. Squeeze the juice of a whole lemon, for you will need it all.

Mix the rest of the spiced sugar with bread crumbs made from the crusts you cut off, and place atop the dish. Grate the peel of the lemon over it. Add ¼ cup of water and the rest of the lemon juice. Dot with butter or margarine.

Bake in a moderate oven, 300 degrees, for 30 minutes with cover on, then brown 10 minutes with cover off.

Serve with a lump of vanilla ice cream on top, or heavy cream if you can get it. This will serve 4. I might have said 5, but this is so delicious you should serve generous portions.

INDEX

Index

(Individual recipes are capitalized)